RAND NATIONAL DEFENSE RESEARCH INSTITUTE

U.S. Department of Defense Experiences with Substituting Government Employees for Military Personnel

Challenges and Opportunities

Jennifer Lamping Lewis, Edward G. Keating,
Leslie Adrienne Payne, Brian J. Gordon, Julia Pollak,
Andrew Madler, H. G. Massey, Gillian S. Oak

Prepared for the Office of the Secretary of Defense
Approved for public release; distribution unlimited

For more information on this publication, visit www.rand.org/t/RR1282

Library of Congress Cataloging-in-Publication Data
ISBN: 978-0-8330-9301-1

Published by the RAND Corporation, Santa Monica, Calif.

Preface

The Director, Total Force Planning & Requirements, Office of the Under Secretary of Defense, Personnel and Readiness (OUSD[P&R]), asked the RAND Corporation to undertake a study titled "Facilitating Military-to-Civilian Conversions." The objective of this research project was to identify the primary impediments to converting military positions to government civilian positions and to recommend changes to statutes, policies, and/or business practices that would facilitate these conversions. The project also examined past experiences with converting military positions and the research literature to identify lessons that could be used to inform future efforts. The RAND team identified a number of opportunities for improving both policies and business practices in order to facilitate military-to-civilian conversions and motivate greater use of this force management tool, should that be the department's goal.

This research should be of interest to Department of Defense personnel involved with manpower planning, civilianization, and managing the trade-offs between military and civilian personnel. It should also be of interest to the makers of laws and policies that govern performance of work by military service members, civilian personnel, and contractors. The research was sponsored by OUSD(P&R) and conducted within the Forces and Resources Policy Center of the RAND National Defense Research Institute, a federally funded research and development center sponsored by the Office of the Secretary of Defense, the Joint Staff, the United Combatant Commands, the Navy, the Marine Corps, the defense agencies, and the defense Intelligence Community.

For more information on the RAND Forces and Resources Policy Center, see www.rand.org/nsrd/ndri/centers/frp or contact the director (contact information is provided on the web page).

Contents

Figures

Tables

Summary

As budget pressures persist for the federal government, the U.S. Department of Defense (DoD) continues to seek ways to gain efficiencies and reduce costs. Optimizing the DoD workforce offers promising opportunities for savings—one aspect of which is determining the right mix of personnel. More specifically, the question at hand is this: How can the department most cost-effectively distribute responsibilities among military service members, civilian personnel, and contracts for services? One force-shaping tool at the department's disposal is the ability to convert military positions to positions filled by federal civilian employees—referred to as military-to-civilian conversions.

The research discussed in this report considers DoD's past and current experience with military-to-civilian conversions to help inform the department's decisions on future use of this force-shaping tool. The research does not address whether the department *should* convert additional positions; instead, it examines the most effective ways to do so. Within that context, the objectives of this research project were to

- examine past experience with converting military positions to identify lessons that can inform future efforts
- identify the primary impediments to converting positions from military to civilian provision
- recommend changes to statutes, policies, and/or business practices that would facilitate these conversions.

The RAND research team employed a multimethod approach in conducting its assessment that included (1) a review of statutes and policies governing performance of work by military service members, government civilian employees, and contractors; (2) an analysis of the most recent experience with military-to-civilian conversions, during fiscal years (FYs) 2004–2012, using Defense Manpower Data Center (DMDC) data; and (3) discussions with human resource, manpower, and budget experts across DoD who have experience with military-to-civilian conversions. The analysis focused primarily on conversions that would be filled by federal civilian employees, and, because of data limitations, it does not include a detailed examination of the potential use of contracts for services. The findings and recommendations summarized here are the result of a synthesis of these research threads.

Governing Policies

The Secretary of Defense is directed in statute to determine the "most appropriate and cost efficient mix" of personnel to accomplish DoD's mission.[1] But other policies and statutes limit the department's ability to make personnel decisions based purely on mission effectiveness and cost considerations. For example, there are many guidelines, statutes, and policies that prescribe ceilings on personnel in various organizations throughout the department. In particular, DoD has capped the number of civilian positions within the Office of the Secretary of Defense (OSD) and the services at FY 2010 levels.[2] Moreover, Congress requires reductions in the total funding for the civilian and contractor workforces that are not less than the savings achieved from reductions in military end strength.[3] In addition, the services are prohibited by statute from reducing the number of military personnel in medical positions below specified thresholds or from converting any medical or dental position from military to civilian provision.[4]

In spite of these constraints, statutes and policies leave a significant amount of room for making subjective judgments about the functions to be performed by military service members, civilian personnel, and contractors. Such leeway grants commanders a fair amount of authority and judgment in managing the workforces in their installations—which is appropriate given their detailed understanding of the specific workings of their installations. The drawback of granting such leeway, however, is that commanders are also able to protect positions from conversion to civilian positions for reasons other than mission effectiveness and cost.

While there is considerable opportunity to pursue military-to-civilian conversions, there appear to be few statutes and policies that offer specific guidance on the process for executing authorized conversions. Existing policies provide abundant guid-

---

1 10 U.S. Code (U.S.C.) 129(a), *General Policy for Total Force Management.*

2 Secretary of Defense, *Department of Defense (DoD) Efficiency Initiatives*, memorandum, August 16, 2010a; U.S. Government Accountability Office, *Critical Skills and Competency Assessments Should Help Guide DOD Civilian Workforce Decisions*, Washington, D.C., GAO-13-188, 2013b; U.S. Congress, House of Representatives, Committee on Armed Services, *Civilian Workforce Requirements—Now and Across the Future Years Defense Program*, hearing before the Subcommittee on Readiness of the Committee on Armed Services, House of Representatives, One Hundred Twelfth Congress, second session, July 26, 2012, Washington, D.C.: U.S. Government Printing Office, 2013.

3 Public Law 112-239, *National Defense Authorization Act for Fiscal Year 2013*, January 2, 2013.

4 10 U.S.C. 129(c), *Medical Personnel: Limitations on Reductions*, amended by Public Law 111-84, *National Defense Authorization Act for Fiscal Year 2010*, Section 701, October 28, 2009, and Public Law 110-181, *National Defense Authorization Act for Fiscal Year 2008*, Section 721, January 28, 2008.

ance on identifying positions for conversion, as well as programming and budgeting the conversions identified. However, the RAND team found little guidance on executing conversions. The process is necessarily complicated because it involves synchronizing military assignments with the civilian hiring process. Hence, the development of such guidance, either by DoD or the services, may prove useful in facilitating military-to-civilian conversions.

Past Experience

The RAND team analyzed DMDC data on civilian and military personnel in an effort to better understand DoD's experience during the previous wave of conversions that occurred between 2004 and 2012. These estimates yielded a number of interesting insights. First, the opportunity to identify positions suitable for military-to-civilian conversion is considerable, since a sizable share of military personnel vacate their positions every year. Our estimates indicate that turnover among military personnel is nearly three times as high as it is among government civilians. These results suggest that civilian personnel provide more continuity than military personnel and reduce training requirements—two reasons why commanders may find value in their civilian employees.

Second, both the number of converted positions and the number of occupations that experienced conversions varied greatly across the services. Our estimates find that almost three-fourths of September 30, 2012, Air Force military personnel worked in occupations in which the Air Force had military-to-civilian conversions over the time period FY 2004–2012. In contrast, about half of September 30, 2012, Army military personnel worked in occupations in which the Army had military-to-civilian conversions over the FY 2004–2012 period.

Over the same time frame, the services typically achieved military-to-civilian conversion substitution ratios around 70 percent, meaning that seven government civilians moved into positions that were previously held by ten military service members. This figure roughly aligns with a 2013 report by the Congressional Budget Office (CBO) that discussed the option of converting 70,000 positions from military to civilian provision over four years at a ratio of approximately two government civilians for every three military service members.[5] The substitution ratios we estimated varied across the services and over time, ranging from 56.8 percent to 88.5 percent.

Military-to-civilian conversions are comparatively unusual relative to the ongoing, large-scale turnover in military positions. Very few positions vacated by military personnel are converted to civilian positions. Most vacated military positions are simply filled by other military personnel. The vast majority of military positions that

---

[5] CBO, *Options for Reducing the Deficit: 2014 to 2023*, Washington, D.C., Pub. No. 4664, November 2013.

are vacated and not filled by other military service members simply remain vacant; we refer to these as "vacated-and-not-filled military positions." Our analysis did not reveal whether the underlying authorizations still exist.

When examining occupations, some experienced no conversions—not surprisingly, combat-oriented occupations, such as missile guidance and control and aircraft launch equipment, fall into this category. Other occupations, most notably security guards (DoD occupation code 1070), experienced so many conversions that they are now filled entirely by civilian personnel. Most occupations exhibited some conversions, but for the vast majority of these, military personnel still dominate the workforce. These occupation categories provide opportunities for additional conversions.

Impediments to Authorizing and Executing Military-to-Civilian Conversions

A question of particular interest to DoD is why so few military-to-civilian conversions are undertaken. What impediments stand in the way of making greater use of this tool? RAND discussed this question with human resource, manpower, and budget experts across DoD who have had experience with military-to-civilian conversions. A revealing outcome of these discussions is that authorizing conversions is not sufficient; for a multitude of reasons, some conversions that are planned and authorized are not executed. Hence, efforts to improve the process must consider not only the factors that impede the *authorization* of military-to-civilian conversions but also the factors that impede the *execution* of authorized conversions. The most salient impediments to military-to-civilian conversions are described below.

Civilian Positions Are More Vulnerable to Cuts Than Military Positions Are

Service-level processes for reviewing proposed conversions are siloed by appropriation, with little coordination between the analysts reviewing the military personnel budget and the analysts reviewing the operation and maintenance (O&M) budget. Consequently, proposing military-to-civilian conversions exposes installations to the risk of losing military personnel without securing the means to hire new civilians.

Even when additional O&M funds are granted for the hiring of civilian replacements, installations may find themselves constrained by civilian full-time equivalent (FTE) ceilings. One expert described a situation in which "the FTE cap stopped hiring. . . . 650 positions that are funded cannot be filled due to the FTE cap." Hiring freezes precipitated by sequestration or other budget-related issues further constrain the hiring of civilians to fill converted positions.

Commanders are concerned first and foremost about having sufficient personnel to cover the workload at their installations. The perception that civilian positions are more vulnerable to cuts than military positions are creates a disincentive to converting positions, even if the move would be more efficient.

Some Military Positions Are Inappropriately Shielded from Conversion

Not all positions can or should be converted to civilian positions. For example, some positions that are classified as military essential, such as infantry and fighter pilots, cannot be converted—nor should they be.

However, there are other positions that perhaps should be considered for civilian provision but are protected as a matter of policy. 10 U.S.C. 129(c), for instance, prohibits the services from reducing the number of uniformed military personnel in medical positions below specified thresholds or from converting any medical or dental position from military to civilian provision.[6] The prohibition on conversions is without exception: Medical and dental positions may not be converted even if the conversions can be shown to reduce costs without compromising access to or quality of care. Several subject matter experts described such restrictions as counterproductive.

Still other positions are shielded from civilianization for reasons of culture and/or tradition. Some commanders prefer military personnel because they obey commands and can work long hours without overtime pay. In other cases, there is simply a prevailing comfort level that results from seeing certain positions, such as recruiting and entry control point positions, staffed with uniformed service members. Ambiguities in policy facilitate shielding such positions from conversion. Installations may appeal to such considerations as esprit de corps, career development, or sea-to-shore rotation to justify the preservation of particular military positions when, in some cases, the justification is inappropriate.

Local Commanders Perceive Military Personnel to Be Free from Cost

Military personnel appropriations funding is managed at the service level. In contrast, O&M funding, which covers the cost of civilian personnel and contracts for services, as well as a number of other items, is managed by the installation. This funding distinction causes installations to treat military personnel as "free" relative to civilian personnel, providing an incentive for commanders to obstruct military-to-civilian conversions. One subject matter expert noted, "The incentive is to keep as much military as you can. If there is a function you want to get, your first try is to use military personnel to do it because they are free."

The issue is exacerbated by the programming and budgeting processes, which do not permit installations to tie the surrender of a military position to an equivalent increase in O&M funds to cover the cost of a civilian replacement. If installations were able to "cash in" a military position in exchange for the means to hire a new civilian, the price of military personnel would, in effect, be set equal to the forgone O&M funds, and local commanders would internalize the trade-off between military and

---

[6] 10 U.S.C. 129(c), *Medical Personnel: Limitations on Reductions*, amended by Public Law 111-84, *National Defense Authorization Act for Fiscal Year 2010*, Section 701, October 28, 2009, and Public Law 110-181, *National Defense Authorization Act for Fiscal Year 2008*, Section 721, January 28, 2008.

civilian personnel. The siloing by appropriation inherent in the current system stymies the establishment of such a link and incentivizes installations to resist military-to-civilian conversions.

A related issue arises from differences between the cost to DoD and the cost to the federal government as a whole. Active-duty service members cost less to DoD because a significant portion of their costs is borne by other federal agencies, such as the Department of Veterans Affairs, the Department of the Treasury, the Office of Personnel Management, and the Department of Education. In contrast, civilian personnel cost more to DoD because few of their costs are borne by other federal agencies and because their higher taxable incomes, while generating larger tax payments to the Treasury, do not count as offsetting receipts to DoD.[7]

Civilian Candidates May Not Be Available to Fill Converted Positions

Well-qualified civilians must be available in the surrounding area and willing to assume the challenges and responsibilities required of a converted position. In some cases, authorized conversions are not executed due to a lack of civilian candidates who have the requisite abilities and experience and are willing to work in a military environment. Identifying a suitable civilian candidate is particularly challenging when the position is located in a remote area or requires special skills. Civilian neurosurgeons, for example, are unlikely to seek employment in rural areas.

Advance analysis of the local labor market can help by providing an estimate of the prevalence of civilians with the requisite qualifications and competencies. However, the two-year lag between the time when conversions are programmed and budgeted and the time when conversions are executed mitigates the relevance of the labor market analysis and magnifies the risk of failing to hire suitable civilian replacements. One expert described such an instance: "The initial market analysis showed we had folks in the area with those skills, but when we went to get them, they were not there."

The sluggishness and rigidity of the civilian hiring process were frequently cited as aggravating factors. The hiring process may not be initiated until the funds to support the new civilian hire have been appropriated. From that point, it may take three to six months to fill the position. A few subject matter experts reported that delays worsened in cases when a large number of civilians had to be hired at one time.

Practical Guidance on the Process for Executing Authorized Conversions Is Sparse

Existing policies provide abundant guidance on determining the optimal workforce mix, identifying positions for conversion, and programming and budgeting the conversions identified. Less attention is paid to the process for executing authorized conversions, and our discussions revealed a general lack of familiarity with the process.

---

[7] CBO, *Replacing Military Personnel in Support Positions with Civilian Employees*, Washington, D.C., Pub. No. 51012, December 2015.

Most subject matter experts reported that they were not aware of any policy documents or guidance relating to the process for executing military-to-civilian conversions. One expert associated with the Navy stated, "A lot of the problem was that there [were] not a lot of good documented policies and no good written guidance on how to execute conversions." This individual reported reaching out to the other services for guidance. "We coordinated to learn from them."

Clearly written, practical guidance on the process for executing military-to-civilian conversions could reduce the confusion described by subject matter experts. The tangible benefit would likely be a reduction in the lag time between authorization and execution, which would reduce the frequency of failed executions. The guidance could be developed by either the department or the services; we are agnostic on this point. The objective is simply to provide practitioners with a clear path from authorization to execution.

Despite these impediments, most of the subject matter experts with whom we spoke voiced general support for an increased role for civilians in DoD. Military commanders valued the experience and continuity that civilian personnel bring to the workplace. In addition, many DoD civilian employees have prior military experience and, as such, are accustomed to working in a military environment. Manpower analysts in the services and OSD recognized that, in most cases, civilian personnel cost less than military personnel or contractors. Many of them favored military-to-civilian conversions as a means of capturing cost savings.

Recommendations

Our research highlights opportunities for Congress, OSD, and/or the services to improve statutes, policies, and business practices in order to facilitate military-to-civilian conversions and motivate greater use of this force management tool, should that be DoD's goal. In addition, we offer a few steps for the department's consideration, should a new wave of military-to-civilian conversions commence.

Changes to Statutes

- **Repeal the prohibition on converting medical and dental positions.** Section 701 of the FY 2010 National Defense Authorization Act prohibits the services from converting any medical or dental position from military to civilian provision, even if the conversion can be shown to reduce costs without compromising access to or quality of care.[8] Several subject matter experts reported that there is

---

8 10 U.S.C. 129(c), *Medical Personnel: Limitations on Reductions*, amended by Public Law 111-84, *National Defense Authorization Act for Fiscal Year 2010*, Section 701, October 28, 2009, and Public Law 110-181, *National Defense Authorization Act for Fiscal Year 2008*, Section 721, January 28, 2008.

ample opportunity for conversions of medical personnel but that very few such conversions are approved because of the statutory restriction. Repealing the prohibition would permit the services to staff medical and dental positions with the "most appropriate and cost efficient mix" of military and civilian personnel, as directed by 10 U.S.C. 129(a).

- **Amend Section 955 to exclude increases in civilian personnel funding that result from cost-effective military-to-civilian conversions.** Section 955 of the FY 2013 National Defense Authorization Act mandates reductions in civilian personnel and contractor expenditures that are commensurate with reductions in funding for basic military pay achieved from reductions in military end strengths. The statute does provide for certain exclusions, but there is no allowance for military-to-civilian conversions that raise civilian personnel expenditures but reduce the overall cost of personnel, both military and civilian.

Changes to Policies

- **Relax the civilian FTE ceilings to exclude civilian positions arising from cost-effective conversions.** Over half of the subject matter experts with whom we spoke cited civilian FTE ceilings as a significant impediment to military-to-civilian conversions. In some cases, the caps have thwarted the execution of conversions that were both authorized and funded. In other cases, installations have refrained from identifying positions for conversion to avoid losing the positions altogether once they are civilianized. Relaxing the civilian FTE ceilings would facilitate the execution of authorized conversions and provide local commanders with appropriate incentives for identifying positions for conversion.
- **Develop clearer, more precise definitions for the military essential criteria.** Installations can argue that certain positions qualify as military essential by appealing to such considerations as esprit de corps, career development, and sea-to-shore rotation. In some cases, subjectivity in determining whether these criteria apply has enabled the protection of military positions for reasons other than mission effectiveness and cost. Eliminating such room for interpretation entirely is likely not possible—or desirable. Local commanders have a more detailed understanding of the specific workings of their installations and should be able to exercise some authority and judgment in managing their workforces. Nevertheless, OSD should explore ways to tighten the definitions of the military essential criteria, such as tying the career development and rotation criteria to appropriate metrics.
- **Issue practical guidance addressing the process for executing authorized conversions.** Existing policies provide abundant guidance on the criteria used to identify positions for conversion and the process for programming and budgeting the conversions identified. However, practical guidance on the process for execut-

ing authorized conversions is sparse. Reducing process ambiguities may shorten the elapsed time between authorization and execution of conversions, increase the likelihood of executing conversions that have been authorized, and improve the experience of commanders and managers engaged in implementing conversions.
- **Develop a clear definition of military-to-civilian conversion and stipulate that data reporting across the services be consistent with that definition.** The data analysis revealed a gap between authorized conversions and executed conversions. In some cases, the gap appears to be artificial—a consequence of inconsistent practices in the reporting of military-to-civilian conversions. Inconsistencies in measuring and reporting conversions impede effective tracking and analysis.

Changes to Business Practices

- **Amend the programming and budgeting processes to permit installations to tie the surrender of a military position to a compensating increase in O&M funds.** Service-level processes for reviewing proposed conversions are siloed by appropriation, with little coordination between the analysts reviewing the military personnel budget and the analysts reviewing the O&M budget. Consequently, proposing military-to-civilian conversions exposes installations to the risk of losing military personnel without securing the means to hire new civilians. Savings from converting positions are captured by the service at large but not by the installations, which regard military personnel as being free from cost. Permitting installations to tie the surrender of a military position to a compensating increase in O&M funds would better align the incentives of the installation with the incentives of the service as a whole.
- **Reduce the time between authorization and execution of conversions.** In order to increase the likelihood that authorized conversions are realized, the services must shorten the time that elapses between authorization and execution. These delays are driven primarily by the two-year lag between the time when conversions are programmed and budgeted and the time when funds are appropriated, the sluggishness and rigidity of the civilian hiring process, and general confusion about the process for executing authorized conversions. Process improvements addressing these root causes may be driven by written guidance, changes to business practices, or both.
- **Conduct an assessment of the local market for civilian labor before authorizing conversions.** The assessment should provide information about the availability of qualified and willing candidates for the civilian positions that will become available and should account for the two-year lag between the time when conversions are programmed and the time when funds are appropriated. Excessive delays between authorization and execution should be avoided so that the conversions can be executed before market conditions change. Our discussions with

subject matter experts indicated that these assessments are frequently, but not always, conducted, and, in some cases, the quality of the assessment is poor.

- **Leverage personnel data to identify occupations or installations that could yield additional conversions.** Analysis of personnel data may be able to provide answers to a number of relevant questions, including: Which occupations have experienced conversions in the recent past? Are there additional military personnel in these occupations that could also be replaced with civilian personnel? Are there occupations in which conversions are prevalent for one service but not for another service?
- **Improve and standardize data collection on contracts for services.** A limitation of the data analysis we conducted is that the data set covered military and government civilian personnel only; comparable data for contractors were not available. As a result, our analysis does not speak to conversions into or out of contractor provision. Improved and standardized data collection on contracts for services would enable a more complete analysis of workforce mix—providing insight on where and in which occupations contractors have been used to perform functions that were previously assigned to military personnel.

Looking Ahead

- **Ensure that estimates of the cost savings associated with military-to-civilian conversions reflect substitution ratios that are feasible in practice.** A 2013 CBO report presented the option of converting 70,000 positions over four years at a ratio of two government civilians for every three military service members to achieve savings of approximately \$20 billion.[9] Our analysis suggests that such a ratio can be implemented on average. However, implementing this ratio may not be feasible in every case. Conversion ratios that are applicable when a large number of similar conversions occur simultaneously may not be practical when only one or two similar conversions occur at a time. DoD, CBO, and other organizations engaged in forecasting cost savings should account for such practical realities when developing estimates.
- **Plan for increased resistance to conversions if the conversions are designed to reduce military end strength.** Military-to-civilian conversions that occurred between FY 2004 and FY 2010 were designed to make military personnel available for deployment. If the next wave of conversions is designed to reduce military end strength instead (as discussed by CBO), then OSD should plan for increased resistance by the services. Stronger guidance—perhaps in the form of targets for military-to-civilian conversions—may be necessary to achieve desired goals. Analysis of personnel data could be used to inform such guidance.

---

[9] CBO, 2013.

Acknowledgments

We thank Richard Robbins, Director, Total Force Planning & Requirements, Office of the Under Secretary of Defense, Personnel and Readiness, for his sponsorship of this research. We also thank Kirstin Austin and Thomas Hessel for serving as points of contact on this research project.

RAND staff spoke with a number of subject matter experts whose time, insights, and participation we greatly appreciate. We specifically thank Charles Denmark of the United States Air Force; Cheryl Cotton, Donna Geren, Michael Iwai, Jamie Karbacka, Ann McClung, and James McDonner of the United States Navy; and Curt Smolinsky and Michael Strobl of the Office of the Secretary of Defense.

We also thank Adebayo Adedeji and Matthew Goldberg of the Congressional Budget Office and Gregory Parton of the United States Air Force for their assistance.

Our RAND colleagues Charles Nemfakos and Daniel Tremblay provided ongoing insights and suggestions on this research project. John Winkler provided guidance as the Forces and Resources Policy Center director. We also appreciate the efforts of Lance Lindauer, Michael Mattock, and Marilyn Yokota, who provided valuable assistance with Human Subjects Protection Committee requirements and Department of Defense second-level review.

We received constructive reviews of an earlier version of this report from Stanley Horowitz of the Institute for Defense Analyses as well as from our RAND colleagues Shanthi Nataraj and Al Robbert. Sarah Meadows orchestrated the RAND National Defense Research Institute quality assurance process.

Abbreviations

AF/A1M	Air Force Directorate of Manpower, Organization, and Resources
AFSC	Air Force Specialty Code
AR	Army Regulation
BES	Budget Estimate Submission
CAPE	Office of Cost Assessment and Program Evaluation
CBO	Congressional Budget Office
CLSWP	Command-Level Strategic Workforce Planning
DMDC	Defense Manpower Data Center
DoD	U.S. Department of Defense
DoDD	Department of Defense Directive
DoDI	Department of Defense Instruction
FAIR	Federal Activities Inventory Reform
FTE	full-time equivalent
FY	fiscal year
G-3	Office of the Deputy Chief of Staff for Operations and Plans
GAO	U.S. Government Accountability Office (known as the U.S. General Accounting Office until 2004)
GS	General Schedule
IDA	Institute for Defense Analyses

MACOM	major command
MCO	Marine Corps Order
MS-3	Manpower Staffing Standards System
NDAA	National Defense Authorization Act
O&M	operation and maintenance
OFPP	Office of Federal Procurement Policy
OMB	Office of Management and Budget
OPNAV	Office of the Chief of Naval Operations
OPNAV N1	Office of the Deputy Chief of Naval Operations for Manpower, Personnel, Training, and Education
OPNAV N12	Total Force Manpower, Training, and Education Requirements Division
OSD	Office of the Secretary of Defense
OUSD(P&R)	Office of the Under Secretary of Defense, Personnel and Readiness
PAPA	Pay and Personnel Ashore
POM	Program Objective Memorandum
REDUCE	Rebalance for an Effective Defense Uniformed and Civilian Employees
TFSP	Total Force Structure Process
U.S.C.	United States Code
USMC	United States Marine Corps

CHAPTER ONE

Introduction

Three broad categories of individuals provide labor services to the U.S. Department of Defense (DoD): government-employed civilians, officer and enlisted military personnel, and contractors. Most cost-benefit analyses conclude that the government should continue to use these sources because "each category of personnel provides unique advantages and belongs in the workforce mix."[1] However, the benefits and costs of these personnel categories differ, and those differences influence the functions best performed by each category of personnel.

Among these categories, military labor is generally thought to be the most expensive on a per-worker basis. In addition to the current pay provided to military personnel, DoD spends millions of dollars per year recruiting and training military members and accrues sizable retirement liabilities for military members who serve for 20 or more years. Health care costs for members of the military, their families, and military retirees are also considerable. Contracts for services can also be costly, but they generally do not involve a long-term commitment by the department. In most cases, it is more difficult to dismiss military or civilian personnel than to terminate a contract.

On an annual basis, government-employed civilians are probably the least costly, though it is more difficult to trim the government-employed civilian labor force than to end a contract. Although the government does face some of the same costs for civilian and military personnel, such as retirement liabilities, the costs of government-employed civilians remain lower overall.[2]

---

1 Beth J. Asch and John D. Winkler, *Ensuring Language Capability in the Intelligence Community: What Factors Affect the Best Mix of Military, Civilians, and Contractors?* Santa Monica, Calif.: RAND Corporation, TR-1284-ODNI, 2013.

2 For analyses of the relative costs of different types of personnel, see Adele R. Palmer and David J. Osbaldeston, *Incremental Costs of Military and Civilian Manpower in the Military Services*, Santa Monica, Calif.: RAND Corporation, N-2677-FMP, 1988; Adele R. Palmer, James H. Bigelow, Joseph G. Bolten, Deena Dizengoff, Jennifer H. Kawata, H. G. Massey, Robert Petruschell, and Michael G. Shanley, *Assessing the Structure and Mix of Future Active and Reserve Forces: Cost Estimation Methodology*, Santa Monica, Calif.: RAND Corporation, MR-134-1-OSD, 1992; and Susan M. Gates and Albert A. Robbert, *Comparing the Costs of DoD Military and Civil Service Personnel*, Santa Monica, Calif.: RAND Corporation, MR-980-OSD, 1998.

DoD Instruction (DoDI) 7041.04 includes a sample cost comparison for a Department of the Army operations research analyst position in the Washington, D.C., metropolitan area, working at a government site.[3] The example shows that the full cost to the government of a General Schedule–14 (GS-14) civilian would be about 25 percent lower than that of an O-5 Army officer (lieutenant colonel), and 10 to 25 percent lower than that of a private contractor. A recent study by the Congressional Budget Office (CBO) finds that, on average, a DoD civilian in a commercial position costs the federal government as a whole about 30 percent less, on an annualized basis, than a military service member in a similar position.[4]

However, per-worker costs are not the only consideration. For example, military personnel tend to vacate their positions more frequently than civilian personnel do.[5] Civilians are therefore able to gain more experience, develop deeper subject knowledge, and provide greater continuity. As a result, fewer civilians are required to achieve a given level of readiness, and fewer civilian accessions are needed to sustain a civilian force of a given size. Civilians also have fewer collateral duties and, therefore, tend to be more available. Finally, civilians sometimes have better training; because they are often recruited to perform a specific function based on their existing skills, civilian employees often begin the position with more or better training relative to their military counterparts, which can, in turn, reduce the training costs borne by DoD. These advantages of civilian manpower may be less pronounced in career fields where civilian recruitment and retention are weak or in career fields where the pay and advancement opportunities are more attractive in the private sector. In cases where the government faces similar difficulty in recruiting and retaining high-quality civilians as it does in developing experienced military personnel, the benefits of conversions may be limited.[6]

Of course, civilians lack some of the advantages of military personnel. Military personnel have military-specific knowledge and skills; can be deployed in dangerous situations, when necessary; and provide commanders with flexibility and a valuable surge capability that civilians cannot provide.[7] Civilians also lack the flexibility of con-

---

[3] U.S. Department of Defense, Department of Defense Instruction 7041.04, *Estimating and Comparing the Full Costs of Civilian and Active Duty Military Manpower and Contract Support*, 2013.

[4] CBO, *Replacing Military Personnel in Support Positions with Civilian Employees*, Washington, D.C., Pub. No. 51012, December 2015.

[5] We provide evidence for this claim in Chapter Three.

[6] For a discussion of the difficulties the government faces in creating a high-quality civilian cybersecurity workforce, see Martin C. Libicki, David Senty, and Julia Pollak, *Hackers Wanted: An Examination of the Cybersecurity Labor Market*, Santa Monica, Calif.: RAND Corporation, RR-430, 2014.

[7] In recent years, civilian deployments have become more common. However, the total number of deployed civilians as a share of the DoD civilian workforce remains quite small. For an end-to-end review and analysis of DoD civilian deployment, see Molly Dunigan, Todd Nichols, Michael Schwille, Susanne Sondergaard, and Susan S. Everingham, *Expeditionary Civilians: Creating a Viable Practice of Civilian Deployment Within the Department of Defense*, Santa Monica, Calif.: RAND Corporation, RR-975-OSD, 2016.

tractors, who enable the government to meet requirements for short-run work or for highly specialized skills—without long-term commitments.[8]

When determining which workers will perform various functions, workers from any of the three categories can fill a considerable number of positions. Yet some functions can only be provided by specific categories of workers. For instance, some roles are defined as *military essential*. Only military members are authorized to use lethal force in military operations on behalf of the U.S. government. There are also some *inherently governmental* positions that require exercising discretion in applying government authority or using value judgment in making decisions for the government.[9] Only government-employed civilians and military members can hold inherently governmental positions.

As budget pressures continue, DoD is interested in better understanding the savings that can be gained by optimizing the use of its labor force—that is, how the department can most cost-effectively distribute responsibilities among military service members, civilian personnel, and contracts for services. Prior research has shown that considerable cost savings can be attained from converting positions currently filled by military service members to positions that can be filled by civilians[10]—often referred to as *military-to-civilian conversions*—but how the government goes about identifying those positions and conducting the transition can affect whether potential savings are ultimately realized.

In 2013, a CBO report discussed the option of replacing "70,000 of the more than 500,000 uniformed military personnel in commercial jobs with 47,000 civilian employees" over four years and estimated that these replacements "could reduce the need for appropriations by $20 billion and for discretionary outlays by $19 billion from 2015 through 2023."[11] To inform DoD's decision on whether to implement this approach and to more aggressively expand military-to-civilian conversions generally,

---

[8] Federal government employees, including DoD civilian personnel, may be hired using temporary or term appointments. Temporary appointments last one year or less and carry a specific expiration date. Term appointments last between one and four years and are used to staff specific projects that are nonpermanent in nature. However, temporary and term appointments are relatively uncommon within the DoD civilian workforce. Of the 704,121 DoD civilians working on September 30, 2015, less than 5 percent were on temporary or term appointments.

[9] Albert A. Robbert, Susan M. Gates, and Marc N. Elliott, *Outsourcing of DoD Commercial Activities: Impacts on Civil Service Employees*, Santa Monica, Calif.: RAND Corporation, MR-866-OSD, 1997; and Jessie Riposo, Irv Blickstein, Stephanie Young, Geoffrey McGovern, and Brian McInnis, *A Methodology for Implementing the Department of Defense's Current In-Sourcing Policy*, Santa Monica, Calif.: RAND Corporation, TR-944-NAVY, 2011.

[10] See Stanley A. Horowitz, *Potential Savings from Substituting Civilians for Military Personnel (A Presentation)*, Alexandria, Va.: Institute for Defense Analyses, IDA Document NS D-5193, 2014; John E. Whitley, Brandon R. Gould, Nancy M. V. Huff, and Linda Wu, *Medical Total Force Management*, Alexandria, Va.: Institute for Defense Analyses, IDA Paper P-5047, 2014; Gates and Robbert, 1998; and Palmer and Osbaldeston, 1988.

[11] CBO, *Options for Reducing the Deficit: 2014 to 2023*, Washington, D.C., Pub. No. 4664, November 2013.

the Office of the Under Secretary of Defense, Personnel and Readiness (OUSD[P&R]), asked the RAND National Defense Research Institute to explore the use of military-to-civilian conversions in DoD. The objectives of this research project were to

- examine past experience with converting military positions to identify lessons that can inform future efforts
- identify the primary impediments to converting positions from military to civilian provision
- recommend changes to statutes, policies, and/or business practices that would facilitate these conversions.

This research focuses on positions currently held by military service members that could instead be filled by government-employed civilians. Because of data limitations, the research does not include detailed examination of the potential use of contracts for services.[12] Moreover, the scope of the research is limited to describing recent experiences with military-to-civilian conversions and identifying impediments to conversions. The research does not take a position on whether military-to-civilian conversions *should* occur.

To conduct this study, the RAND research team employed a multimethod approach:

- review of relevant statutes and policies governing performance of work by military service members, government civilian personnel, and contractors
- analysis of the most recent experience with military-to-civilian conversions based on data provided by the Defense Manpower Data Center (DMDC)
- discussions with human resource, manpower, and budget experts across DoD who have experience with military-to-civilian conversions.

In addition, we conducted a review of relevant literature to identify best practices for selecting an appropriate mix of personnel. The review is intended to provide context and serve as a baseline against which to compare the results of our independent assessment (see Appendix A).

This report describes the insights and recommendations that result from the various components of research. In Chapter Two, we begin with an overview of statutes, directives, and instructions pertaining to workforce conversions in DoD. What are the legal constraints on military-to-civilian conversions? What administrative instructions have been promulgated? Chapter Three reports findings from an empirical analysis of when, where, and in what functions military-to-civilian conversions have occurred. This DMDC-based analysis suggests that not all authorized military-to-civilian con-

[12] The amount of data available to understand and analyze military and government-employed civilian labor is much greater than the data available on where and how contractors are used in DoD.

versions have actually been executed. The analysis also identifies civilian-to-military conversions—cases in which military personnel appear to have assumed positions previously held by DoD-employed civilians. In Chapter Four, based on discussions with subject matter experts, we detail the process by which military positions are converted to government civilian positions and identify the most salient impediments to authorizing and executing military-to-civilian conversions. Finally, Chapter Five offers recommendations for changes that Congress, the Office of the Secretary of Defense (OSD), and/or the services could make to statutes, policies, and business practices that would facilitate military-to-civilian conversions, should DoD choose to increase this practice.

CHAPTER TWO

An Overview of Statutes, Directives, and Instructions

To gain an understanding of the legal drivers of military-to-civilian conversions, as well as the laws and policies that constrain these conversions, we examined federal, DoD, and military service policy documents. In many cases, these policy documents were not specifically written to address conversions, but instead were directives on such topics as the development of an appropriate workforce mix or ensuring that essential tasks were not delegated to contractors. In total, we reviewed over 70 documents and identified 37 that were relevant to the issue of military-to-civilian conversions. These policy documents include applicable statutes, DoD guidance, and instructions from each of the services.[1]

Statutes and Government-Wide Directives

The category of statutes and government-wide directives includes any policy that is put forth by Congress or a responsible federal agency that applies to all federal activities. Those policies promulgated by Congress include parts of Titles 5 and 10 of the United States Code (U.S.C.), National Defense Authorization Acts (NDAAs) of various fiscal years, and public laws. Government-wide directives include Circular A-76 from the Office of Management and Budget (OMB), which concerns public-private competitions, and Letter 11-01 from the Office of Federal Procurement Policy (OFPP), which addresses inherently governmental and critical functions. These directives from Congress and other government agencies establish procedures for determining the optimum mix for an agency's workforce, rules for determining whether contractor support

[1] To identify relevant documents, we reviewed Department of Defense Directive (DoDD) 1100.4 and DoDI 1100.22, both of which had extensive reference lists that included relevant DoDIs and related documents (located using the Defense Technical Information Center) and statutes (located from the Government Printing Office website and the website of the Legal Information Institute of Cornell Law School). We used official websites of the military services to identify relevant service instructions: Army Publishing Directorate, Department of the Navy Issuances, the U.S. Air Force e-publishing website, and the Marine Corps Publications Electronic Library. In addition, we conducted web searches using relevant terms, such as "military to civilian," and searched the reference lists in the many instructions identified.

is appropriate, and instances in which special circumstances apply that necessitate a departure from normal practice.

Optimum Workforce Mix

Over 50 percent of the relevant policy directives provide guidance on establishing the optimum workforce mix within an organization. These directives address the number and types of personnel that make up the organization—the number of personnel that can be employed; required reports that justify the number of military, civilian, and contractor positions; and rules for cost-benefit decisions. Chief among these is 10 U.S.C. 129(a), which directs the Secretary of Defense to determine the "most appropriate and cost efficient mix" of personnel required to accomplish DoD's mission.[2] Additional clarification in 10 U.S.C. 129(b) specifies that developing the appropriate mix for mission accomplishment takes precedence over cost.[3]

Additionally, several statutes mandate reports to Congress on the status of the DoD workforce. Pentagon officials are required to develop and submit an annual Defense Manpower Requirements Report and a biannual Strategic Workforce Plan.[4] The requirements report links recommended DoD manpower levels to national security objectives. It also provides detail on the manpower requirements for the medical missions of each of the services and information on the demographics of each service's promotion and recruiting activities. The Strategic Workforce Plan is a five-year plan that sets strategic guidance for each of DoD's functional communities and outlines the necessary measures to establish and maintain core competencies across the workforce.

In establishing the requirements for an optimum mix of military service members, government civilian personnel, and contracts for services, DoD must take into account manpower restrictions on some categories of personnel as prescribed by such vehicles as NDAAs, congressional statutes, and administration directives. Some of these personnel restrictions are defined by organization, such as the ceiling on the total number of personnel (military and civilian) that can be assigned to OSD.[5] Others limit the number of personnel performing a function, such as headquarters management.[6]

Inherently Governmental Functions

When considering the role of contractors, there is considerable guidance on specific functions that are sufficiently related to the public interest that they are reserved for military and federal civilian personnel—functions referred to as *inherently governmental.*

---

[2] 10 U.S.C. 129(a), *General Policy for Total Force Management.*

[3] 10 U.S.C. 129(b), *Authority to Procure Personal Services.*

[4] 10 U.S.C. 115(a), *Annual Defense Manpower Requirements Report*; and 10 U.S.C. 115(b), *Biennial Strategic Workforce Plan.*

[5] 10 U.S.C. 143, *Office of the Secretary of Defense Personnel: Limitation.*

[6] 10 U.S.C. 194, *Limitations on Personnel.*

There are two sources for policies related to inherently governmental functions. The first is the Federal Activities Inventory Reform (FAIR) Act of 1998, which defines an inherently governmental function as "a function so intimately related to the public interest as to require performance by Federal Government employees."[7] A second, slightly looser definition comes from OMB Circular A-76, which defines *inherently governmental* as "an activity so intimately related to the public interest as to mandate performance by government personnel."[8]

In addition, some specific functions are defined as inherently governmental in the statutes that mandate their performance. The requirement for each agency to submit a strategic plan to Congress and OMB each year carries with it the restriction that these plans should be drafted by federal employees because the task is considered inherently governmental.[9] The effect of these various statutes and policy documents is to create a group of functions that, regardless of cost, benefit, or other considerations, will only be performed by military and federally employed civilian personnel.

OFPP 11-01 is the primary reference used by DoD. It clarifies what functions are inherently governmental, provides guidance on how to manage work that is "closely associated" with inherently governmental functions, and identifies "critical functions" that should be filled by federal employees in order for an agency to "effectively perform and maintain control of its operations."[10] The critical functions identified include monitoring contractors and support to the DoD workforce. The effect of this guidance is to expand the well-defined set of "federal only" functions to include additional ones that may be more subject to interpretation.

Public-Private Competition

For those functions that are outside the definition of inherently governmental, statutes and policies addressing public-private competition influence workforce determination—in particular, OMB Circular A-76, most recently revised in May 2003. This circular specifies that functions that are not inherently governmental must be identified by agencies annually and opened up to competition with private sources. The intent of this policy is to ensure efficiency and cost-effectiveness throughout each agency. These functions can remain in the hands of federal employees, but the agency must determine that it is better suited to perform the function itself. However, because of concerns about the competitive process and overuse of contract support, Congress placed a moratorium on these competitions. DoD public-private competitions under OMB

---

[7] Public Law 105-270, *Federal Activities Inventory Reform Act of 1998*, October 19, 1988.

[8] OMB, Circular A-76 (Revised), 2003.

[9] 5 U.S.C. 306, *Agency Strategic Plans.*

[10] OMB, Office of Federal Procurement Policy, *Policy Letter 11-01—Performance of Inherently Governmental and Other Critical Functions*, Federal Register, Vol. 76, No. 176, 2011, pp. 56227–56229.

Circular A-76 were suspended by the NDAA for fiscal year (FY) 2008.[11] A government-wide moratorium was instituted with the passage of the Omnibus Appropriations Act for FY 2009[12] and has been extended through FY 2016.[13] As a result of this moratorium, DoD is statutorily prohibited from shifting work currently performed by military and civilian personnel to contractors.

Incongruities and Exceptions

As written, the statutes that direct the formulation of an efficient and cost-effective workforce mix, define inherently governmental functions, and mandate public-private competitions are clear in their direction. But because of operational or political requirements, policymakers have modified these policies, normally through additional legislation. The Circular A-76 moratorium is one example of an exception to the overall theme of establishing a cost-effective, optimum workforce mix.

10 U.S.C. 129(c) provides the additional restriction that, for any fiscal year, the Secretary of Defense may not reduce the number of uniformed medical personnel below specified thresholds unless the Secretary makes a certification for that fiscal year that both of the following conditions apply:[14]

1. The number of medical personnel being reduced is excess to the current and projected needs of DoD.
2. Such reduction will not result in an increase in the cost of health care services provided under the Civilian Health and Medical Program of the Uniformed Services.

Moreover, conversions of medical and dental positions from military to civilian provision have been prohibited since October 1, 2007.[15] The prohibition is without exception: Medical and dental positions may not be converted even if the conversions can be shown to reduce costs without compromising access to or quality of care.

Section 955 of the FY 2013 NDAA mandates reductions in civilian personnel and contractor expenditures that are commensurate with reductions in compensation paid to military personnel. More specifically, the act requires that the Secretary of Defense develop and execute an "efficiencies plan" that achieves savings in total funding for the civilian and contractor workforces over the period FY 2012–2017 that "are

---

[11] Public Law 110-181, *National Defense Authorization Act for Fiscal Year 2008*, January 28, 2008.

[12] Public Law 111-8, *Omnibus Appropriations Act, 2009.*

[13] Public Law 114-113, *Consolidated Appropriations Act, 2016*, December 28, 2015.

[14] 10 U.S.C. 129(c), *Medical Personnel: Limitations on Reductions.*

[15] 10 U.S.C. 129(c), *Medical Personnel: Limitations on Reductions*, amended by Public Law 111-84, *National Defense Authorization Act for Fiscal Year 2010*, Section 701, October 28, 2009, and Public Law 110-181, *National Defense Authorization Act for Fiscal Year 2008*, Section 721, January 28, 2008.

not less, as a percentage of such funding, than the savings in funding for basic military personnel pay achieved from reductions in military end strengths" over the same period.[16] Section 955 provides for certain exclusions, but the overall effect of the statute is to hinder shifts in the workforce mix from military personnel to civilian personnel and contracts for services—even when these shifts are cost-effective.

Other exceptions are less obvious because they result from separate policies. For example, DoD officials are permitted by statute to designate civilian positions as "emergency essential" if the task being performed is necessary to support combat operations.[17] While not directly addressing the issue of optimal workforce mix, this designation is an exception to that guidance. Though the job may be more adequately, appropriately, or cost-effectively filled with a military member, the "emergency essential" designation permits keeping a civilian in the role to ensure continuity of operations.

DoD Instructions

The direction promulgated in the approximately 20 relevant statutes identified in this research is codified within DoD by only a handful of broad instructions and directives. The first of these is DoDD 1100.4, *Guidance for Manpower Programs*. The intent of this document is to ensure that DoD objectives are accomplished with "a minimum of manpower that is organized and employed to provide maximum effectiveness and combat power,"[18] evoking 10 U.S.C. 129(a). In addition to referencing and quoting the applicable statutes directly, DoDD 1100.4 defines additional requirements for manpower policy that are specific to DoD. Among them are ensuring that workforce mix decisions are made with consideration of career progression opportunities and personnel rotations. Each of the services issues similar guidance specific to its mission and personnel system (discussed further in the following section).

The second principle source of guidance on manpower decisions comes from DoDI 1100.22, *Policy and Procedures for Determining Workforce Mix*. As with DoDD 1100.4, some of this instruction codifies statutory guidance for the DoD audience. Concepts such as "inherently governmental functions" are defined according to the higher-level guidance of the FAIR Act, Circular A-76, and OFPP 11-01. But DoDI 1100.22 gives more specific guidance on the topic of military/civilian workforce mix. It directs that, consistent with DoDD 1100.4, manpower will be designated as civilian

---

16 Public Law 112-239, *National Defense Authorization Act for Fiscal Year 2013*, January 2, 2013.

17 10 U.S.C. 1580, *Emergency Essential Employees: Designation*.

18 DoDD 1100.4, p. 2.

unless the function to be performed is *military essential*—that is, unless one or more of the following conditions are relevant:[19]

- Military-unique knowledge and skills are required.
- Military incumbency is required by law, executive order, treaty, or international agreement.
- Military performance is required for command and control, risk mitigation, or esprit de corps.
- Military manpower is needed to provide for overseas and sea-to-shore rotation, career development, or wartime assignments.
- Unusual working conditions or costs are not conducive to civilian employment.

Additionally, the enclosures of DoDI 1100.22 include criteria for determining inherently governmental functions and visual depictions of the manpower mix decision process. Guidance for risk assessments that may influence decisions about military and civilian manpower is included in enclosure (5) of DoDI 1100.22.

The DoD-level guidance put forth in DoDD 1100.4 and DoDI 1100.22 translates statutory requirements into specific guidance for DoD and each of the services. For many of the service-level instructions, these DoD documents are the applicable references, rather than the statutes from which the policies are drawn. They are, therefore, important links between the intent of Congress and other federal organizations and the realities of how each part of DoD addresses the issues of workforce mix.

Additional DoD-level guidance bearing on workforce mix has been promulgated via memoranda issued by OSD. Of particular relevance to the issue at hand are the civilian full-time equivalent (FTE) caps imposed in FY 2010. On August 16, 2010, the Secretary of Defense issued a memorandum directing the department to freeze (or cap) the number of civilian positions within OSD, the defense agencies, the field activities, the Joint Staff, and the Combatant Commands at FY 2010 levels through FY 2013.[20] Four days later, the Secretary provided additional guidance authorizing the Deputy Secretary of Defense to grant exceptions to the civilian personnel caps "on a component basis, for compelling circumstances."[21] Resource Management Decision 703A2 extended the civilian workforce caps to the military services on January 25,

---

19 DoDI 1100.22, p. 3.

20 Secretary of Defense, *Department of Defense (DoD) Efficiency Initiatives*, memorandum, August 16, 2010a.

21 Secretary of Defense, *Guidance on DoD Efficiency Initiatives with Immediate Application*, memorandum, August 20, 2010b.

2011.[22] The following year, the caps were extended through FY 2018.[23] Despite the numerous exceptions that have been granted,[24] civilian workforce caps impede shifts in the workforce mix from military to civilian personnel—even in cases in which the shift generates cost savings, and funds are available to cover the cost of civilian hires.[25]

Service Instructions

Each of the services issues specific guidance for determining workforce mix, using the DoD-level instructions as references. While these instructions are largely consistent with the DoD guidance, each service addresses concerns specific to its mission and culture and, in some cases, issues guidance that may be open to interpretation. Additionally, each service takes a unique approach as to what level of the organization is responsible for these manpower issues.

Army

In the Army, a primary document for analyzing workforce decisions is Army Regulation (AR) 570-4, *Manpower Management*, which "implement[s] DoDD 1100.4, *Guidance for Manpower Programs*."[26] The regulation designates the authority and responsibility for determining manpower mix, establishes procedures for analyzing manpower requirements, and specifies reporting requirements. It states that Army policy is to (1) design units with the appropriate mix of military service members, government civilian personnel, and contracts for services to provide full mission capability, and (2) use the least costly mix of manpower consistent with military requirements and other needs of the Army.[27]

AR 570-4 also addresses methodologies for analyzing the workforce. The Manpower Staffing Standards System (MS-3) is identified as the Army's tool for developing manpower requirements through work measurement and directs both functional area

---

22 U.S. Government Accountability Office (GAO), *Critical Skills and Competency Assessments Should Help Guide DOD Civilian Workforce Decisions*, Washington, D.C., GAO-13-188, 2013b.

23 U.S. Congress, House of Representatives, Committee on Armed Services, *Civilian Workforce Requirements—Now and Across the Future Years Defense Program*, hearing before the Subcommittee on Readiness of the Committee on Armed Services, House of Representatives, One Hundred Twelfth Congress, second session, hearing held July 26, 2012, Washington, D.C.: U.S. Government Printing Office, 2013.

24 GAO, 2013b.

25 We provide evidence for this claim in Chapter Four.

26 Department of the Army, AR 570-4, *Manpower Management*, 2006, p. 1.

27 Department of the Army, 2006, p. 12.

staff components and those at major commands (MACOMs) to use MS-3 when determining their desired mix of personnel.[28]

On the subject of military-to-civilian conversions, AR 570-4 delegates significant authority to the MACOMs in making personnel decisions. The regulation states that "civilian substitution programs" can maintain or reduce military end strength by substituting civilians for military personnel on a one-to-one basis. MACOMs have authority under this regulation to institute such programs.[29] In addition, MACOMs' force managers are able to convert positions from military to civilian if the conversion is within existing civilian strength levels. If such an action is outside strength levels, the MACOM "must compete for resources through the normal budget process."[30] The conversion process does not work in reverse, however. The same chapter emphasizes that civilian-to-military conversions (except for abolishment of positions) can only occur if the job is recategorized through normal processes, which entails approval by the U.S. Army Force Management Support Agency.[31]

The Army has several methods for analyzing organizational work patterns and workforce composition that are described and mandated in AR 570-4. But the bulk of the analysis and development of workforce mix, including conversions, is delegated to the MACOMs by this regulation.

Navy

The Navy also has a primary document for addressing workforce mix: the Office of the Chief of Naval Operations (OPNAV) Instruction 1000.16L, *Navy Total Force Manpower Policies and Procedures*. This instruction is promulgated by OPNAV and does not address Marine Corps issues. With regard to military-to-civilian conversions, the instruction describes conversions as an important part of reducing military authorizations in nonoperational functions. Billets identified for potential conversion by the Office of the Deputy Chief of Naval Operations for Manpower, Personnel, Training, and Education (OPNAV N1) are designated in the Total Force Manpower Management System, with the Total Force Manpower, Training, and Education Requirements Division, N12, being the designated official for policy, guidance, and oversight of manpower requirements.[32] Military essentiality requirements that conform with DoD instructions are listed, as are additional requirements that can justify designating a position as military. These additional requirements include maintenance of sea-to-shore rotation, educational and career progression

28 Department of the Army, 2006, p. 17.

29 Department of the Army, 2006, p. 28.

30 Department of the Army, 2006, p. 33.

31 Department of the Army, 2006, p. 34.

32 OPNAV, OPNAV Instruction 1000.16L, *Navy Total Force Manpower Policies and Procedures*, 2015, p. 4-1.

assignments, and preservation of a sufficient number of billets to ensure adequate military personnel for wartime-only assignments.[33] Finally, the instruction includes an explanation of inherently governmental requirements and civilian requirements, such as continuity of infrastructure operations during a national emergency and core logistics capability.[34]

Air Force

The Air Force promulgates manpower and workforce mix guidance through two key documents. The first is Air Force Policy Document 38-2, *Manpower,* which references both DoDD 1100.4 and DoDI 1100.22 and establishes the policy through which the Air Force will identify manpower requirements and resources.[35] The document establishes Unit Manpower Documents as the means by which the Air Force allocates manpower resources. The A1 section of the Air Staff is designated as the responsible office for defining analytically based manpower requirements and managing the Unit Manpower Documents.

The second and broader document is Air Force Instruction 38-201, *Management of Manpower Requirements and Authorizations*, which is the Air Force counterpart to OPNAV Instruction 1000.16L and AR 570-4. This instruction implements policy on determination of manpower requirements, workforce mix, and mission essentiality. It describes manpower as "a limited resource which is sized to reflect the minimum essential level to accomplish the required workload."[36] This instruction includes a workforce mix flowchart and a table for determining military essentiality that synthesizes DoD guidance.[37] It also designates the Air Force Directorate of Manpower, Organization, and Resources (AF/A1M) with the responsibility for determining military essentiality for all billets.[38]

Though Air Force Instruction 38-201 is the primary instruction for workforce management, the Air Force seems to have several established methodologies by which manpower managers can determine their workforce mix. One such methodology is the Air Force Management Engineering Program, a framework for developing manpower standards and analysis tools to determine the minimum essential manpower required to accomplish a mission. This program is defined by Air Force Manual 38-208 (Volumes

---

33 OPNAV, 2015, p. 2-4.

34 OPNAV, 2015, p. 2-5.

35 Office of the Secretary of the Air Force, Air Force Policy Document 38-2, *Manpower*, March 2, 1995.

36 Office of the Secretary of the Air Force, Air Force Instruction 38-201, *Management of Manpower Requirements and Authorizations,* 2014, p. 11.

37 Office of the Secretary of the Air Force, 2014, pp. 105–106.

38 Office of the Secretary of the Air Force, 2014, p. 22.

I–III), which is referenced throughout Air Force Instruction 38-201.[39] Several methods of analysis are referenced in this instruction. Two examples are cost (high-level) analysis and detailed (low-level) analysis.[40] In high-level cost analysis, each process performed by the workforce is assigned a cost based on the total resources associated with it, of which manpower is one. The allocation of resources to various processes in the unit can then be evaluated based on manpower required and manpower assigned. In low-level detailed analysis, frequency and "per accomplishment times" are collected for each process within the unit to give managers a detailed picture of how the workforce is employed and where changes can be made. By describing these and other methods of analysis, the Air Force provides workforce managers with valuable tools to evaluate the efficiency of their organization and manpower mix.

United States Marine Corps

As with the other services, the United States Marine Corps (USMC) has taken guidance from both DoDD 1100.4 and DoDI 1100.22 and promulgated a primary instruction to address the issues pertaining to military-to-civilian conversions—Marine Corps Order (MCO) 12250.2, *Civilian Command-Level Strategic Workforce Planning (CLSWP) Procedures.* The CLSWP is a position-by-position review of the military, civilian, and contractor workforces that both clarifies the organizational structure and reduces redundancy.[41] Though conversions are not specifically addressed, Appendix C of the order does detail workforce requirements projections for the organization over the next five years. This includes removal or modification of positions and addressing gaps, such as inappropriate grade or inappropriate military or civilian status of a position.[42]

Within this order is one point of guidance that is potentially open to interpretation by managers. The order provides a classification scheme for positions according to mission criticality, ranking them as high, medium, or low. High billets are vital to mission success and must "be filled via interim measures (military, civilian, contractor) during ongoing recruitment efforts."[43] This guidance is clear, logical, and within the bounds of statutory and DoD guidance. However, it is conceivable that an organization might classify particular positions as high that other organizations might not and would then fill those positions with available manpower that differs from the military, civilian, or contractor coding for that billet while conducting recruiting. If recruiting is delayed by civilian workforce availability, operational imperatives, or simply the hiring

---

39 Office of the Secretary of the Air Force, 2014, pp. 11–12.

40 Office of the Secretary of the Air Force, 2014, pp. 30–31.

41 Commandant of the Marine Corps, Marine Corps Order 12250.2, *Civilian Command-Level Strategic Workforce Planning Procedures,* 2014, p. 2-2.

42 Commandant of the Marine Corps, 2014, p. C-6.

43 Commandant of the Marine Corps, 2014, p. 2-6.

preferences of the manager, then this guidance may allow the position to be converted for a protracted time period, despite the fact that the conversion is not justified under existing guidance.

Another relevant USMC directive, MCO 5311.1D, *Total Force Structure Process (TFSP)*, details the process by which the development and maintenance of USMC force structure is conducted, directs the identification of resources needed to accomplish mission-essential tasks, and specifically addresses military-to-civilian conversions. The Deputy Commandant for Manpower and Reserve Affairs is directed to chair the Military-to-Civilian Working Group. Commands are directed to submit a list of positions they wish to convert, and those submissions are validated by the TFSP system.[44] In addition, the MCO specifies that for every position created under this system, another position must be removed, so that the total number of positions (both military and civilian) remains unchanged through TFSP. Requests for increases in manpower are submitted through other administrative channels.[45] Additionally, civilian positions cannot be removed in exchange for military positions through TFSP.[46] In sum, the USMC instructions designate a senior-level coordinator for these analyses but place the burden of analysis and argument for force structure on the commands.

Summary

Section 129(a) of Title 10 of the U.S.C. directs the Secretary of Defense to determine the "most appropriate and cost efficient mix" of personnel required to accomplish DoD's mission. Yet other statutes and policies place constraints on the department's ability to make personnel decisions based purely on mission effectiveness and cost considerations. These constraints include the following:

- Civilian personnel are prohibited from performing those functions designated as "military essential."
- Only military and government civilian personnel can perform inherently governmental functions.
- OSD is limited by statute in its total number of personnel (military and civilian).
- Personnel levels for many headquarters and management activities throughout DoD are limited without congressional waiver.[47]

---

44 Commandant of the Marine Corps, Marine Corps Order 5311.1D, *Total Force Structure Process (TFSP)*, 2009, p. 5-9.

45 Commandant of the Marine Corps, 2009, p. 6.

46 Commandant of the Marine Corps, 2009, p. 5-6.

47 These restrictions include 10 U.S.C. 194, which limits the Defense Agencies and DoD Field Activities; 10 U.S.C. 143, which limits the number of OSD personnel; 10 U.S.C. 3014, which limits the Office of the Sec-

- The services may not reduce the number of military personnel in medical positions below specified thresholds or convert any medical or dental position from military to civilian provision.
- Congress requires reductions in the total funding for the civilian and contractor workforces that are not less than the savings achieved from reductions in military end strength.
- Congress placed a moratorium on A-76 competitions, which were previously used to convert military and government civilian positions to contractor provision.
- The Secretary of Defense has capped the number of civilian positions at FY 2010 levels within OSD and the services.

In spite of the constraints outlined above, statutes and policies leave a significant amount of room for making subjective judgments about the functions to be performed by military service members, government civilian personnel, and contractors. For instance, DoDI 1100.22 dictates that positions required for risk mitigation or esprit de corps be filled by military personnel. Positions needed to provide for overseas and sea-to-shore rotation or for career development must also be filled by military personnel. Such leeway grants commanders a fair amount of authority and judgment in managing the workforces in their installations.

There appear to be few statutes and policies that offer specific guidance on the process for executing conversions. Existing policies provide abundant guidance on identifying positions for conversion, as well as programming and budgeting the conversions identified. However, the RAND team found little guidance on the process for executing authorized conversions. The process is necessarily complicated because it involves synchronizing military assignments with the civilian hiring process. Hence, the development of such guidance, either by DoD or the services, may prove useful in facilitating military-to-civilian conversions. We revisit this point in Chapters Four and Five.

---

retary of the Army and the Army Staff; 10 U.S.C. 5014, which limits the Office of the Secretary of the Navy, OPNAV, and the Headquarters, Marine Corps; and 10 U.S.C. 8014, which limits the Office of the Secretary of the Air Force and the Air Staff.

CHAPTER THREE

Insights from Empirically Estimated Military-to-Civilian Conversions

As discussed in Chapter One, a 2013 CBO report presented the option of another wave of military-to-civilian conversions as a means of reducing personnel costs in DoD. We embarked on two parallel paths of research to help DoD determine whether this would be a fruitful course of action and how best to undertake another round of conversions, should that action be desired. First, we analyzed DMDC data on military and civilian personnel in an effort to better understand the effects of the previous wave of conversions, which occurred from FY 2004–2012. We discuss the results of that analysis in this chapter. Second, we spoke with subject matter experts involved in the previous wave of conversions to gather data on impediments to successful military-to-civilian conversion—the topic of Chapter Four.

Data

DMDC collects annual "snapshots" of DoD's military and civilian workforces as of September 30 each year—the last day of the fiscal year.[1] These annual snapshots capture a variety of attributes of DoD's military and civilian personnel—e.g., their rank or grade, their location, and various descriptions of their backgrounds and qualifications. In other words, the data describe specific individuals who either serve in the military or are employed by a military service. This information is distinct from the authorization data that describe positions and the requirements that individuals must have to fill these positions.

We draw attention to the difference between people tracked in the DMDC data (referred to as "faces") and the positions tracked in the authorizations data (referred to as "spaces") because the two can easily be confounded. The issue is further complicated when there is a mismatch between authorized positions and the individuals selected to occupy them. Such a mismatch can occur in a number of ways:

[1] Because no comparable inventory exists for contractors, we were not able to estimate conversions to or from contractor provision.

- A position may be authorized but not filled. In such a case, DMDC data will not include the position because the data track individuals, not positions.
- A position may be filled by an individual who has different characteristics (either grade/rank or qualification) than what was authorized for the position. In this case, DMDC data will include the individual filling the position but will not have information about the mismatch in characteristics.
- A position may be an "over-hire"—i.e., an individual is holding a position that does not appear in the authorizations. DMDC data will not note such a discrepancy.

In this chapter, we will use the term *filled position* or just *position*, but it is important to note that this is a position as seen in the DMDC data—that is, a specific individual with specific characteristics assigned to or working at a specific location on a given September 30.

Our analysis utilizes two key DMDC variables. The first is the *duty zip code*, which identifies the employee's work location. So, for example, an Army employee with duty zip code 76544 works at Fort Hood, Texas. The second, less well-known key variable is termed an *occupational subgroup* by DoD; it is identified by the first four characters of the six-character DoD occupation code.[2] We refer to these first four characters as *DoD occupation codes* throughout the remainder of this document. The first of the four characters in the DoD occupation code is either a 1 or a 2. A 1 denotes a position that would be associated with an enlisted member of the military (or the civilian equivalent, including, for instance, most wage grade employees). A 2 denotes a position that would be associated with commissioned or warrant officers (or the civilian equivalent).

Illustrating some widely used occupation codes, Table 3.1 presents 19 DoD occupation codes that represent the United States Navy's ten most common military and civilian codes on September 30, 2012. DoD occupation code 1551, Supply Administration, was both the ninth most common military code and the ninth most common civilian code in the Navy.

We utilized DoD occupation codes in our analysis because these codes are used for both military and civilian personnel and they exist for all four military services. The services themselves manage their workforces using other variables; for instance, the Air Force uses its Air Force Specialty Codes (AFSCs). However, because our analysis covers all four services, service-specific codes, such as the AFSCs, are of limited value. Table 3.1 illustrates that some DoD occupation codes solely cover military personnel, some solely cover civilians, and others cover both military and civilian personnel.

---

2 DoD, Office of the Under Secretary of Defense, Personnel and Readiness, *Occupational Conversion Index: Enlisted/Officer/Civilian*, DoD 1312.1-1, March 2001.

Table 3.1
Most Common DoD Occupation Codes in the United States Navy Military and Civilian Workforces, September 30, 2012

DoD Occupation Code	Number of Military Personnel	Number of Civilians
Radio/Radar, General, 1100	**12,992**	0
Missile Guidance and Control, 1121	**9,402**	0
ADP Computers, General, 1150	**10,508**	5
Medical Care and Treatment, General, 1300	**26,177**	743
Other Technical Specialists and Assistants, 1496	0	**8,142**
Administration, General, 1510	4,767	**6,730**
Supply Administration, 1551	**8,666**	**5,154**
Aircraft Launch Equipment, 1604	**8,631**	0
Main Propulsion, 1651	**16,199**	1,064
Other Mechanical and Electrical Equipment, General, 1690	0	**6,053**
Law Enforcement, General, 1830	**8,700**	2,389
Not Occupationally Qualified, General, 1950	**13,097**	0
Ground and Naval Arms, 2205	**9,844**	511
Electrical/Electronic, 2402	397	**13,794**
Engineering and Maintenance Officers, Other, 2414	1,023	**13,890**
Mathematicians and Statisticians, 2510	0	**4,700**
Administrators, General, 2701	451	**16,030**
Comptrollers and Fiscal, 2704	0	**6,023**
Data Processing, 2705	816	**9,183**

SOURCES: DMDC Military and Civilian Personnel Inventories.

NOTES: Bold denotes the ten most common codes for military and civilian personnel categories. ADP = automated data processing.

Methodology

Our goal is to empirically estimate military-to-civilian conversions—i.e., instances in which the DMDC military and civilian data suggest that such a conversion has occurred. We looked for cases where a member of the military filled a position (defined by the combination of the zip code and the four-character DoD occupation code) in one year but a service-employed civilian occupied the position the next year. Along with estimating military-to-civilian conversions, we also estimated a smaller number of civilian-to-military conversions—cases where it appears that military personnel have supplanted government-employed civilians.

It is important to understand that the data presented here are *estimates*. We cannot say for certain that a specific position shift represents a military-to-civilian (or civilian-to-military) conversion. Rather, we are tallying cases that appear to be such conversions from a data analysis perspective.

Our methodology makes some critical assumptions. Most notably, we assume that a military-to-civilian (or civilian-to-military) conversion preserves the four-character DoD occupation code and the position's physical location (zip code). If, for instance, a group of civilians in one DoD occupation code replaced a group of military personnel in a different occupation code, our technique would not see that as a military-to-civilian conversion. Rather, it would see military personnel vacating positions in one occupation category and new civilian positions appearing in a different category without drawing any connection between the two events. The same is true if, for some reason, the replacement civilians had a different duty zip code than the military personnel they replaced. Indeed, as we illustrate in the next section, the vast majority of vacated military positions are not filled by civilians; rather, it is far more common for a vacated-and-not-filled military position to be eliminated or left unoccupied.[3] There is nearly continuous change in the functions being performed by and locations of military personnel, independent of any military-to-civilian conversions.

Stepping Through Our Methodology

Our methodology starts by comparing a service's September 30 military personnel inventories in adjacent years. Illustrating the methodology, Figure 3.1 presents Army soldiers as of September 30, 2009 (the bar on the left), and September 30, 2010 (the bar on the right). Figure 3.1 depicts actual human beings identified in the DMDC Military Personnel Inventory, not authorized military positions. Soldiers fall into four categories. A small majority of the personnel are the same soldiers in the same occupations and locations in both FY 2009 and FY 2010 (the blue segment). The next largest slice (the orange segment) is the soldiers holding different occupations and/or in different locations in the Army in FY 2010 compared with FY 2009 (but being in the Army both years). Then we have soldiers who were in the Army in FY 2009 but not in FY 2010 (green segment), and soldiers who were in the Army in FY 2010 but not in FY 2009 (purple segment).

---

3 We refer to a position as being *vacated* if the current holder changed occupation and/or geographic location. We refer to a position as *vacated and not filled* if we could not identify a replacement soldier (for a vacated military position) whom we think replaced the soldier who departed. Because we did not have access to authorization data, we do not know whether a vacated-and-not-filled position remained authorized and not filled or whether the position's authorization had been eliminated.

Figure 3.1
Army Soldiers on September 30, 2009, and September 30, 2010

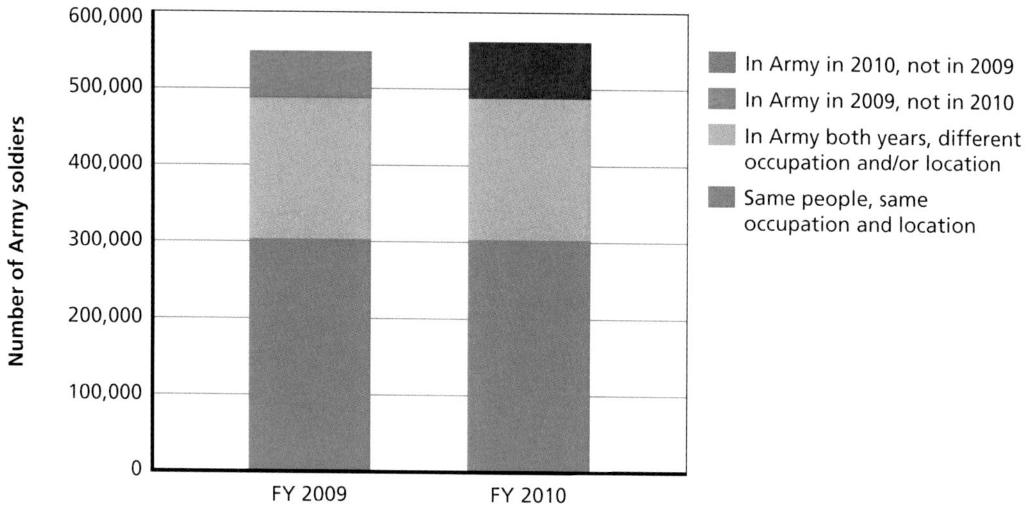

SOURCE: DMDC Military Personnel Inventories.
RAND *RR1282-3.1*

Of the Army positions vacated by military personnel after September 30, 2009 (left orange and green segments), some were filled by different soldiers in FY 2010.[4] We looked at Army personnel new to their positions in FY 2010. Some had been in the Army in FY 2009 but were in a different position (different occupation and/or location) in FY 2010 (right orange segment). Others were new to the Army in FY 2010 (purple segment).

We estimated that a FY 2010 soldier filled a vacated position if we identified a match on duty zip code (e.g., 76544 for Fort Hood, Texas) and four-character DoD occupation code (e.g., 1551 for Supply Administration). We compared individuals that comprise the orange and purple segments of the FY 2010 bar (i.e., soldiers new to their positions in FY 2010) with those in the orange and green segments of the FY 2009 bar (i.e., soldiers who vacated their positions between September 30, 2009, and September 30, 2010). When a match was found on both zip code and occupation code, we counted the FY 2010 individual as having filled the position vacated by the FY 2009 individual.

Our technique suggests a fair amount of turnover in military occupations and locations across all services and years. For example, of 549,020 soldiers in Army positions in FY 2009, we found that

---

[4] As discussed earlier in this section, "position" is defined as the combination of location (i.e., zip code) and occupation (i.e., four-character DoD occupation code) that we observed the soldier occupying.

- 304,652 (55.5 percent) stayed in the same occupation and location in FY 2010
- 179,127 positions (32.6 percent) were held by a different soldier in FY 2010
- 65,241 (11.9 percent) of Army positions in FY 2009 were not filled by a soldier in FY 2010.

Likewise, of 561,983 soldiers in FY 2010 Army positions, we found that

- 304,652 (54.2 percent) had been in the same occupation and location in FY 2009
- 179,127 positions (31.9 percent) had been held by a different soldier in FY 2009
- 78,204 (13.9 percent) of Army positions in FY 2010 were not occupied by a member of the Army in FY 2009.

As noted, we defined a position by the combination of the zip code and the four-character occupation code. So, for instance, when we say that 65,241 Army positions in FY 2009 were not filled by a soldier in FY 2010, we mean that there were 65,241 cases where a soldier holding a particular position in FY 2009 left that position (i.e., changed zip code, occupation code, or both), but we did not observe a soldier in FY 2010 moving into that vacated position. Likewise, in FY 2010, 78,204 Army soldiers were new to their positions (i.e., had a new zip code and/or occupation code), with no match for that position having been vacated in FY 2009.

The DMDC data did not tell us whether the authorization undergirding the vacated-and-not-filled position still existed. It could be that the authorization had been eliminated, or the position could still have been authorized but was no longer filled.

We undertook a similar procedure for Army-employed civilians. Not surprisingly, as shown in Figure 3.2, relative to military personnel, we found that a higher percentage of Army civilians were in the same position in FY 2009 and FY 2010.[5] Figure 3.2 depicts actual human beings in the DMDC Civilian Personnel Inventory, civilian employees of the military services. We found the same pattern of more turnover in military than civilian positions for the other services and in other years. Note, too, that the scale of Army civilian employment is lower than that of military employment. The Army employs roughly one civilian for every two military members.

We were particularly interested in Army civilians in positions in FY 2010 that did not exist in FY 2009. We found 28,330 civilians in these new civilian positions—16,355 of these civilians were new hires by the Army, and 11,975 were employed by the Army in FY 2009 but in a different location and/or occupation.[6] The question, then, is whether any of these new Army civilian positions appear to be positions that were occupied by an Army soldier in FY 2009 but for which we could not find a FY 2010 replacement

[5] As before, "position" is defined as the combination of location (i.e., zip code) and occupation (i.e., four-character DoD occupation code) that we observed the Army civilian occupying.

[6] These are Army civilians in the right orange and purple segments of Figure 3.2 whose location and occupation do not match the location and occupation of any Army civilian in the left orange and green segments of Figure 3.2.

Figure 3.2
Army-Employed Civilian Personnel on September 30, 2009, and September 30, 2010

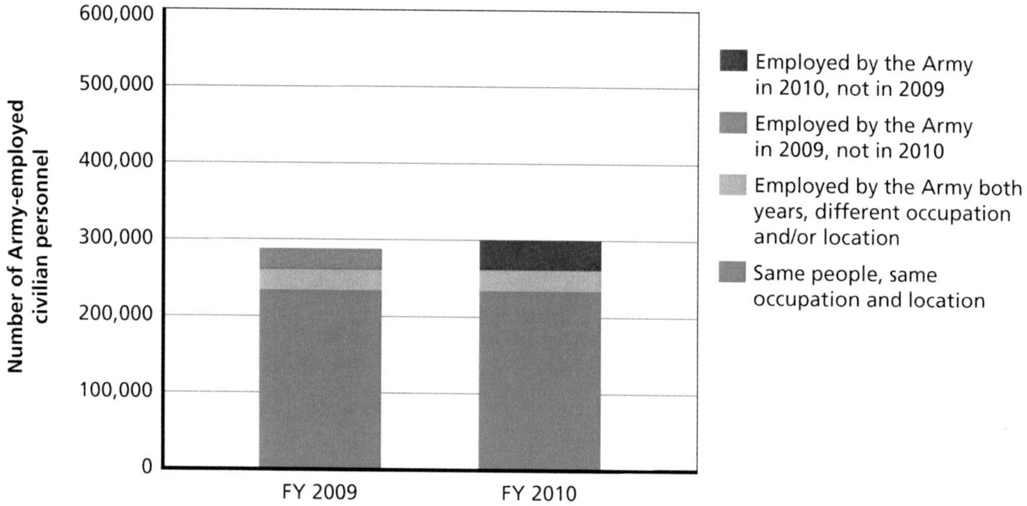

SOURCE: DMDC Civilian Personnel Inventories.
RAND *RR1282-3.2*

soldier—that is, whether we could locate a match on the duty zip code and the four-character DoD occupation code between the new FY 2010 civilian position and the vacated-and-not-filled FY 2009 military position.

Our algorithm sorted through the 28,330 Army-employed civilians in new positions in FY 2010 (i.e., civilian positions that did not exist in the preceding year) to see whether any of these new Army civilian positions matched one of the 65,241 vacated-and-not-filled military positions.[7] For FY 2010, we found 1,084 Army-employed civilians in positions that were held by Army soldiers as of September 30, 2009, but were not filled by a soldier on September 30, 2010. We took a second look at these positions, running the 1,084 Army-employed civilians against the remainder of the vacated-and-not-filled military positions to see whether a second match could occur. It is plausible (and, in fact, presented as common in OSD, 2009) that one civilian might be able to replace more than one military member, in light of the additional responsibilities borne by military members (e.g., physical training, protocol duties). In this case, we located a second match against a vacated-and-not-filled Army soldier position for 526 of the 1,084 FY 2010 Army-employed civilians. Hence, we estimated that 1,084 FY 2010 Army-employed civilians were in positions held by 1,610 Army soldiers in FY 2009—a substitution ratio of 67.3 percent (1,084 divided by 1,610).

---

[7] A match occurs when the location (i.e., zip code) and occupation (i.e., four-character DoD occupation code) of a FY 2010 Army civilian in a new position coincide with the location and occupation of one of the 65,241 FY 2009 soldiers whose position was "vacated and not filled," as defined earlier.

There is another possibility, as noted by one of our reviewers. It could be that some of the functions performed by the 526 military personnel included in our second analysis were, in fact, abandoned or turned over to contractor support. However, our algorithm was structured so as to estimate that the 1,084 new-to-their-positions government-employed civilians replaced all 1,610 (1,084 + 526) military members. In that sense, the algorithm estimates a ceiling on the number of military members replaced by government-employed civilians.

We note that our algorithm was an ex post search for cases in the data that appeared to be military-to-civilian conversions—not a characterization of how DoD decides to make such conversions. The DoD decision to convert a position (instead of maintaining military provision of a function) occurs while the position is still held by a military member. The process of a military member vacating a position, no replacement military member filling it, and then a civilian eventually filling the position is a consequence or symptom of the implementation of the military-to-civilian conversion decision. Our algorithm searched for scenarios that fit that pattern and then labeled these instances as estimated military-to-civilian conversions.

There is an element of arbitrariness to our conversion estimation procedure. We allowed one civilian to possibly replace two, but not more than two, military personnel. We did not, however, allow a military member to replace more than one civilian. As a practical matter, we think that many military-to-civilian conversions involve groups of military personnel and civilians—e.g., seven civilians replace ten military members. Under such a scenario, all seven civilians would match on a vacated-and-not-filled military position, and then an arbitrarily chosen three of the seven civilians would absorb one additional military position each. Because we are ultimately interested in the aggregate count (e.g., seven civilians replace ten military members), it is of no practical importance which three civilians were arbitrarily matched with extra military positions.

Suppose that instead of seven civilians replacing ten military members, seven civilians actually replaced seven military personnel. In such a circumstance, the seven civilians would match against the seven vacated-and-not-filled military positions, but then the second loop would come up empty, as there would be no leftover vacated-and-not-filled military positions. Our algorithm allows for, but does not force, any arbitrary number N civilians to replace as few as N or as many as $2N$ military members.

Using the results of this analysis, we were able to estimate the substitution ratios for each of the services in the FY 2004–2012 time frame, as shown in Table 3.2. A substitution ratio of 100 percent indicates a one-to-one substitution of civilian for military personnel. A substitution ratio of 70 percent means that seven civilians would be in positions held by ten military personnel in the prior year. We found that the services typically achieved military-to-civilian conversion substitution ratios around 70 percent.

Table 3.2
Estimated Military-to-Civilian Conversion Substitution Ratios, FY 2004–2012

Fiscal Year	Air Force	Army	Marine Corps	Navy
2004	71.4%	88.5%	62.1%	75.8%
2005	65.8%	87.0%	58.1%	69.4%
2006	69.9%	80.0%	69.0%	70.4%
2007	69.9%	75.8%	61.0%	66.2%
2008	66.2%	66.7%	68.5%	76.3%
2009	69.4%	71.9%	73.0%	81.3%
2010	71.4%	67.1%	64.5%	78.7%
2011	70.4%	65.8%	56.8%	76.9%
2012	69.9%	69.9%	71.4%	69.0%

NOTE: The substitution ratio equals the number of civilian personnel in a specific position in year *X* divided by the number of military personnel in the same position (matching the four-character occupation code and zip code) in year *X* – 1.

We also consider an additional possibility. Suppose that a position was held by a military member on September 30, 2009, and that he or she left the position during FY 2010, but the position remained vacated and not filled through September 30, 2010, as the civilian hiring process moved forward. It may not be until the September 30, 2011, civilian inventory that we see a replacement civilian in that position. To account for such a possibility, we also compared Army-employed civilians in new positions in FY 2011 against the list of vacated-and-not-filled military positions from FY 2009 (that had not been identified as being filled by a civilian in 2010). We only did so, however, after those FY 2011 civilians in new positions had been compared against the FY 2010 vacated-and-not-filled military positions. We estimated that 61 Army soldier positions as of September 30, 2009, were left unfilled on September 30, 2010, but were filled by Army-employed civilians on September 30, 2011.

This lagged hiring search did not work for the last fiscal year in our data, FY 2012. Because we did not have an inventory beyond September 30, 2012, we could not see any hiring for a position that opened in FY 2012 but was not filled as of September 30, 2012. Consequently, our military-to-civilian estimates for FY 2012 in Figure 3.4 and Table 3.4 likely underestimate the number of conversions relative to other fiscal years.

It is important to put our estimated conversions in context. As illustrated in Figure 3.3, our analysis shows that civilians fill only a small minority of vacated military positions. About three-fourths of vacated military positions are filled by other military personnel. Of the remaining vacated-and-not-filled military positions, the vast majority appear to be left empty. We do not know whether the underlying authoriza-

Figure 3.3
The Relative Infrequency of Military-to-Civilian Conversion, Army, FYs 2009–2010

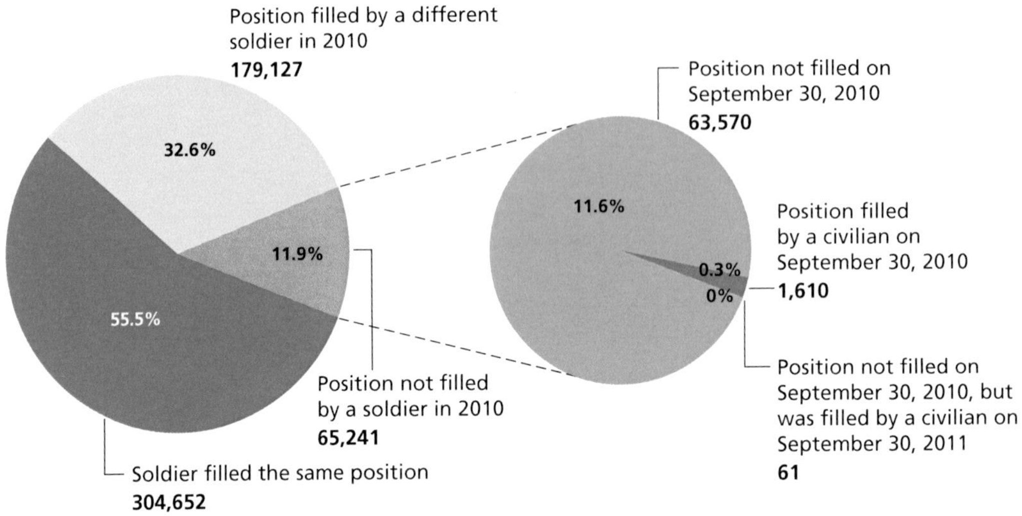

SOURCES: RAND-developed methodology using DMDC Military and Civilian Personnel Inventories.
RAND *RR1282-3.3*

tion continued to exist through September 30, 2010, or beyond. The bottom line is that *military-to-civilian conversion is the exception, not the norm.*

Interestingly, using similar logic, our technique also estimates that there were 622 civilian-to-military conversions in the Army between FY 2009 and FY 2010. These represent Army soldiers in new military positions that appear to be positions given up by Army-employed civilians. (We did not run a second comparison when estimating civilian-to-military conversions because we did not think that it was plausible that a military member might replace more than one civilian.)

Estimates of Military-to-Civilian Conversions

Using the methodology described in the previous section, we estimated military-to-civilian conversions by military service for FYs 2004–2012. The results are illustrated in Figure 3.4. Our estimates show a fairly steady string of military-to-civilian conversions for the Air Force from FYs 2005–2010 which then declined in FY 2011 and FY 2012. The Navy had a surge of military-to-civilian conversions in FY 2007 that fell to pre-FY 2007 levels around FY 2010. The Army had an upturn in military-to-civilian conversions from FYs 2008–2011 but a decline, much like the Air Force, in FY 2012. Because FY 2013 data were not available to complete the second pass through the FY 2012 data, as described earlier in our methodology, these results may underestimate the number of conversions in FY 2012.

Figure 3.4
RAND-Estimated Military Positions Converted to Civilian Provision, FYs 2004–2012

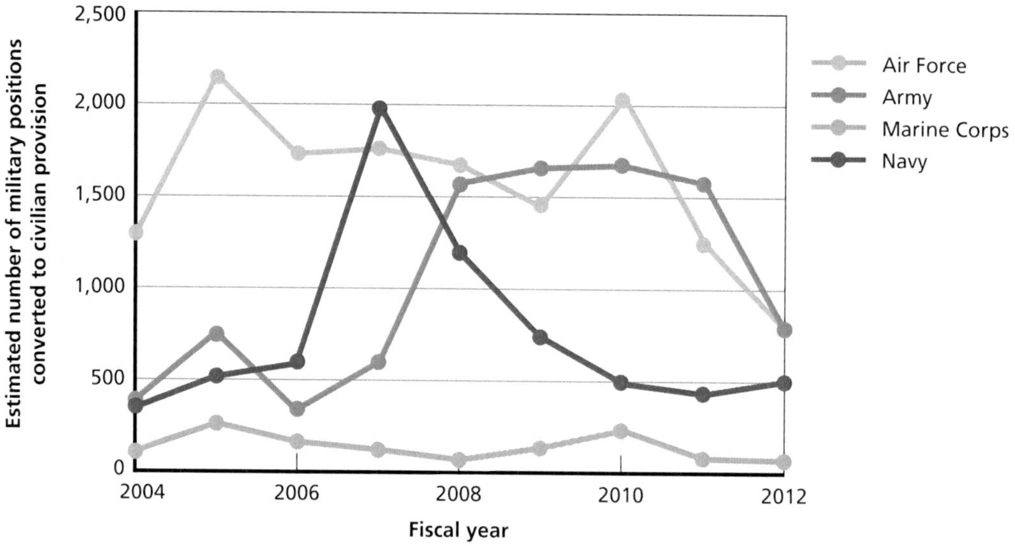

SOURCES: RAND-developed methodology using DMDC Military and Civilian Personnel Inventories.
RAND *RR1282-3.4*

Figure 3.5 shows the percentage of FY 2012 personnel in each of the four services that experienced at least some military-to-civilian conversions in their occupation during FYs 2004–2012. Not surprisingly, some combat-oriented occupations experienced no military-to-civilian conversions—such as Infantry, General (code 1010) and Fixed-Wing Fighter and Bomber Pilots (code 2201). We found that approximately three out of four FY 2012 Air Force military members were in DoD occupation codes that had some military-to-civilian conversion. In contrast, fewer than 40 percent of Marines were in such occupation codes.

Figure 3.6 presents a scatter diagram of those four-character occupations that had any estimated military-to-civilian conversions between FY 2004 and FY 2012. On the horizontal axis, we show the occupation's estimated FYs 2004–2012 military-to-civilian conversions. On the vertical axis, we show the occupation's FY 2012 military strength. Most of the data points plotted are sizably above the horizontal axis, which means that most of the occupations that had military-to-civilian conversions between FY 2004 and FY 2012 still had a large number of military personnel serving in them on September 30, 2012. Figure 3.7 presents a complementary portrayal, with estimated FYs 2004–2012 military-to-civilian conversions on the horizontal axis and the percentage of each occupation's FY 2012 positions held by military personnel on the vertical axis.

Occupations in which conversions had occurred but that still had a large number of military personnel serving in them—data points in the upper center-right portion

Figure 3.5
Percentage of FY 2012 Military Personnel in Four-Character Occupation Codes That Had Military-to-Civilian Conversions in FYs 2004–2012

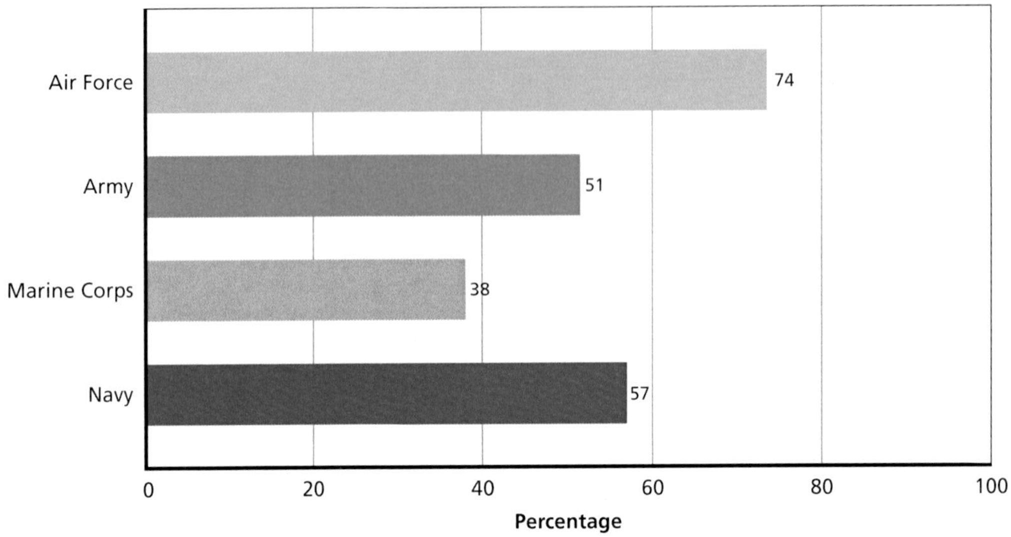

SOURCES: RAND-developed methodology using DMDC Military and Civilian Personnel Inventories.
RAND *RR1282-3.5*

Figure 3.6
Estimated FYs 2004–2012 Military-to-Civilian Conversions and FY 2012 Military Strength by Four-Character Occupation Codes

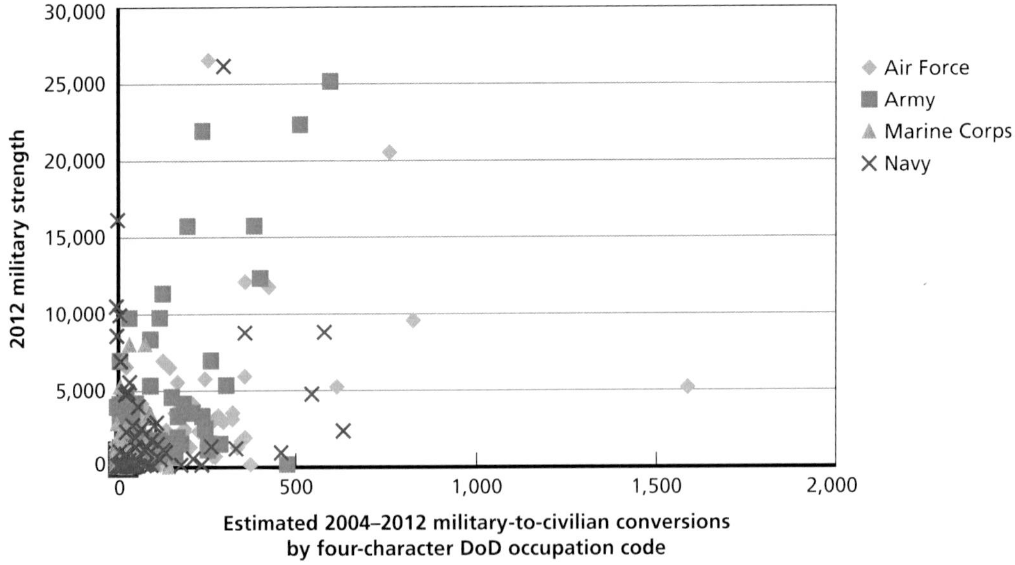

SOURCES: RAND-developed methodology using DMDC Military and Civilian Personnel Inventories.
RAND *RR1282-3.6*

Figure 3.7
Estimated FYs 2004–2012 Military-to-Civilian Conversions and Percentage of FY 2012 Positions Held by Military Personnel, by Four-Character Occupation Codes

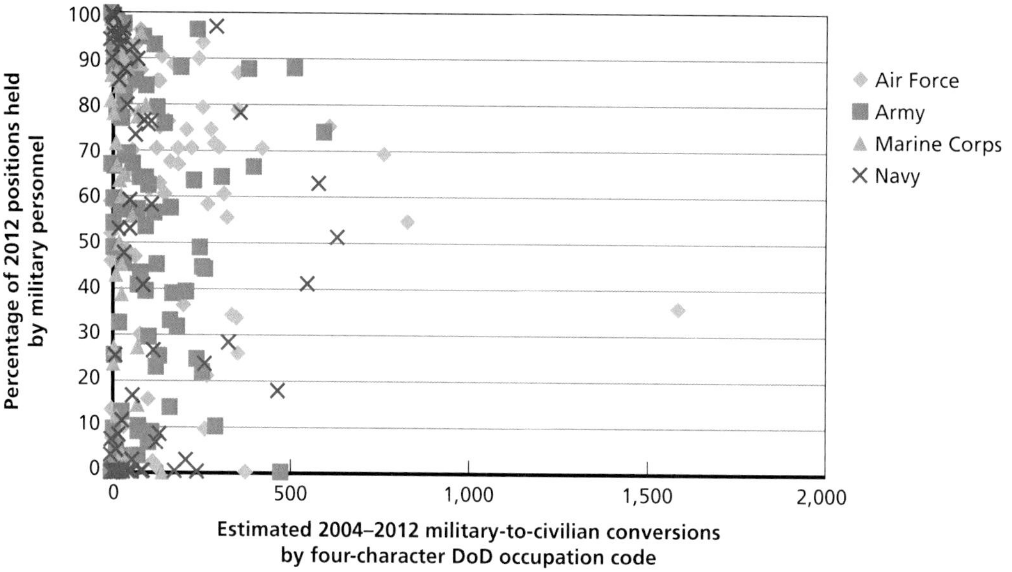

SOURCES: RAND-developed methodology using DMDC Military and Civilian Personnel Inventories.
RAND *RR1282-3.7*

of the figures—would appear to be promising candidates for additional conversions. Occupations to the left in the figures would seem less promising because they have only had a few military-to-civilian conversions (or none on the vertical axis). Occupations in the lower parts of the figures would seem less promising because fewer military slots remain that could be converted. Table 3.3 highlights some of the prominent outlier occupations in Figures 3.6 and 3.7. The first nine rows are occupations that had a sizable number of military-to-civilian conversions but retained thousands of military members as of September 30, 2012. We view these nine occupations as having considerable potential for future military-to-civilian conversions because such conversions have occurred in these occupations, but sizable numbers of military remain in the occupations. Two marked exceptions are presented at the bottom of Table 3.3. The Army no longer has any soldiers serving in military occupation codes that map to Administration, General (code 1510), although the Air Force and Navy still have military personnel in military occupation codes mapping to code 1510. Meanwhile, Security Guards (code 1070) have been completely removed from military provision DoD-wide. This is the lone occupation that had a sizable number of military-to-civilian conversions between FY 2004 and FY 2012 and is now bereft of military personnel.

Table 3.3
Military-to-Civilian Conversion Experience for Selected DoD Occupations

DoD Occupation Code	Component	FY 2004–2012 Military-to-Civilian Conversions	FY 2012 Military Personnel	Percentage of FY 2012 Positions Held by Military Personnel
Administration, General, 1510	Air Force	1,584	5,075	36
Supply Administration, 1551	Air Force	825	9,541	55
Aircraft, General, 1600	Air Force	762	20,568	69
Construction, General, 1710	Navy	634	2,361	32
Personnel, General, 1500	Air Force	610	5,018	75
Supply Administration, 1551	Army	597	25,203	74
Supply Administration, 1551	Navy	577	8,666	63
Administration, General, 1510	Navy	546	4,767	41
Medical Care and Treatment, General, 1300	Army	511	22,451	88
Administration, General, 1510	Army	474	0	0
Security Guards, 1070	Air Force	373	0	0

SOURCES: RAND-developed methodology using DMDC Military and Civilian Personnel Inventories.

Estimates of Civilian-to-Military Conversions

Military-to-civilian conversions are not the whole story. Civilian-to-military conversions—cases in which military service members appear to be filling positions vacated and not filled by service-employed civilians—are also occurring. Table 3.4 reprises Figure 3.4's estimates of the services' military-to-civilian conversions but shows our estimates of the services' civilian-to-military conversions as well. The table suggests that *both types of conversions have been regularly occurring over time.* For the most part, the number of military-to-civilian conversions exceeds the number of civilian-to-military conversions.[8]

There are some occupations that exhibit both military-to-civilian and civilian-to-military conversions. Figure 3.8 shows one of them, Supply Administration (code 1551). This occupation has had concurrent military-to-civilian and civilian-to-military conversions at various locations in the Air Force.

8 In FY 2012, we estimate that more Air Force civilian-to-military conversions than military-to-civilian conversions occurred. However, as discussed previously, our estimate of 2012 military-to-civilian conversions is biased downward because these estimates do not include lagged conversions that were not completed until FY 2013.

Table 3.4
RAND-Estimated Military-to-Civilian and Civilian-to-Military Conversions, FYs 2004–2012

Service	Fiscal Year	Estimated Military-to-Civilian Conversions	Estimated Civilian-to-Military Conversions
Air Force	2004	1,287	757
	2005	2,152	449
	2006	1,721	404
	2007	1,750	685
	2008	1,663	543
	2009	1,439	493
	2010	2,037	461
	2011	1,241	451
	2012	788	825
Army	2004	386	208
	2005	753	448
	2006	335	934
	2007	602	571
	2008	1,565	69
	2009	1,657	465
	2010	1,671	622
	2011	1,574	1,200
	2012	785	758
Marine Corps	2004	109	25
	2005	259	17
	2006	162	48
	2007	118	81
	2008	70	83
	2009	132	29
	2010	228	43
	2011	76	95
	2012	70	70
Navy	2004	340	398
	2005	517	296
	2006	579	161
	2007	1,977	133
	2008	1,184	161
	2009	746	136
	2010	492	177
	2011	424	217
	2012	496	272

SOURCES: RAND-developed methodology using DMDC Military and Civilian Personnel Inventories.

Figure 3.8
RAND-Estimated Air Force Conversions in Occupation 1551, Supply Administration, FYs 2004–2012

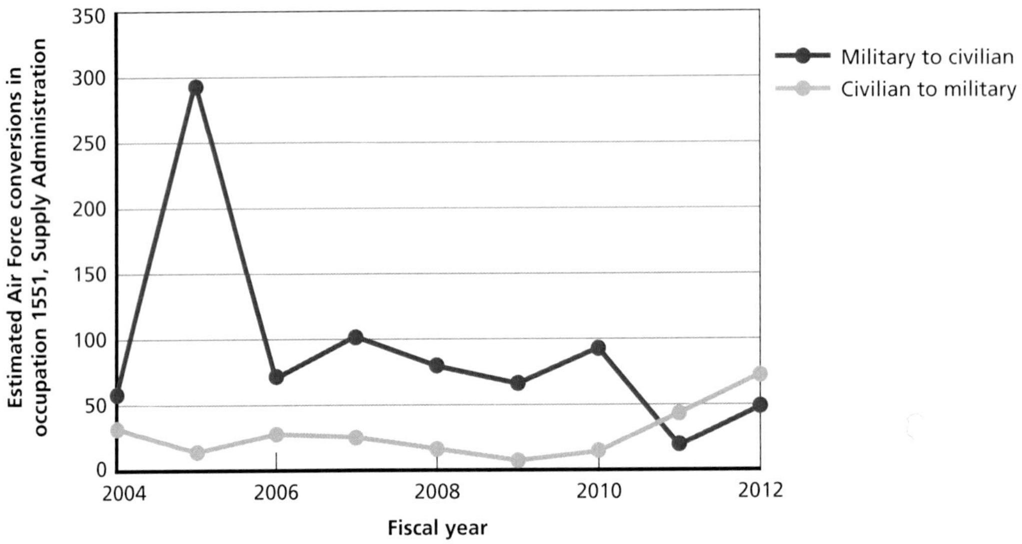

SOURCES: RAND-developed methodology using DMDC Military and Civilian Personnel Inventories.
RAND *RR1282-3.8*

The analysis can be extended to the installation level. Figure 3.9 shows Occupation 1551, Supply Administration, at Eglin Air Force Base in Florida. Eglin has had both military-to-civilian conversions (the bars above the horizontal axis) and civilian-to-military conversions (the bars below the horizontal axis) for this occupation in recent years. Our algorithm estimates so many conversions in both directions because the base's populations of military and civilian personnel in supply administration have been generally negatively correlated—i.e., one population has tended to increase while the other has decreased, as illustrated in Figure 3.10.

Comparing Findings with Authorization-Based Estimates

As noted, DMDC data cover actual human beings in positions. Another way to consider conversions would be to analyze how authorizations for positions change over time. When examining authorizations, it is important to remember that authorized positions are not always filled and are not always filled by individuals with exactly the stipulated qualifications. Nevertheless, it is plausible and logical to expect a connection or correlation between DMDC data on individuals and data on authorized positions. For example, a change in authorizations should be a necessary condition (though not

Figure 3.9
RAND-Estimated Net Military-to-Civilian Conversions in Occupation 1551, Supply Administration, at Eglin Air Force Base, FYs 2004–2012

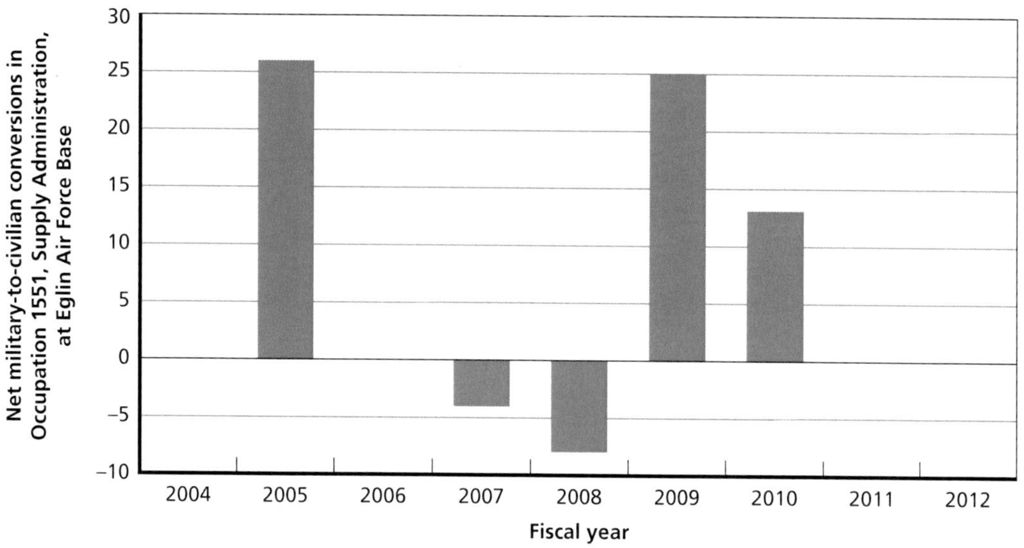

SOURCES: RAND-developed methodology using DMDC Military and Civilian Personnel Inventories.
RAND *RR1282-3.9*

Figure 3.10
Tallies of Air Force Military and Civilian Personnel in Occupation 1551, Supply Administration, at Eglin Air Force Base, FYs 2003–2012

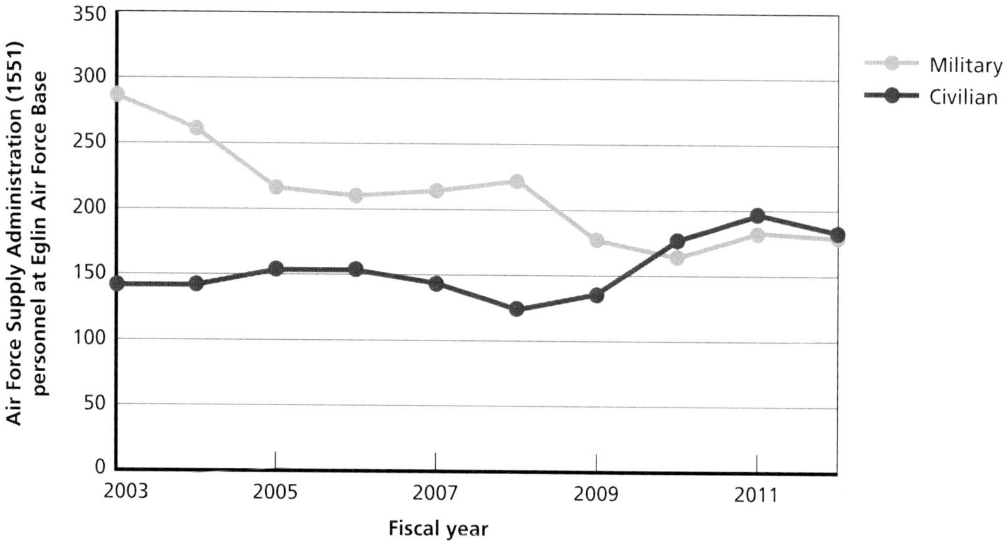

SOURCES: DMDC Military and Civilian Personnel Inventories.
NOTE: The range for these data begins at 2003 instead of 2004 because this figure is based on population data; the other figures estimate conversions based on the differences in population data from year to year.
RAND *RR1282-3.10*

a sufficient one—civilian personnel funding would also be required, for instance) to observe a military-to-civilian conversion in the DMDC data.

We were able to access FYs 2005–2013 Air Force authorization data to compare with our findings from the DMDC data for the Air Force. We developed an algorithm for Air Force authorization data that was similar to our DMDC-based algorithm. In particular, in an attempt to estimate conversions, the algorithm looked for cases in which military authorizations diminished and civilian authorizations increased concurrently within a given zip code–occupation pair. For example, in FY 2007, Dyess Air Force Base (zip code 79607) had 195 military personnel and 26 civilians in authorized positions for Supply Administration (code 1551). In FY 2008, Dyess had 189 military and 27 civilian authorized positions in code 1551. We did not think it plausible that one civilian had replaced six military service members, so we instead estimated that the one additional civilian had replaced two military service members at Dyess in FY 2008 in Supply Administration (code 1551). This approach is similar to the methodology applied to the DMDC data.

As shown in Figure 3.11, our techniques across the two data sets generated similar estimates of Air Force military-to-civilian conversions. The fact that authorization-estimated conversions modestly exceeded DMDC-estimated conversions is not surprising, given that not all authorized conversions have actually been executed. The DMDC and authorization data seem to be particularly in accord as to a downward trend in Air Force military-to-civilian conversions between FY 2010 and FY 2012.

Figure 3.11
A Comparison of Estimates of Air Force Military-to-Civilian Conversions for Individuals and Positions, FYs 2004–2013

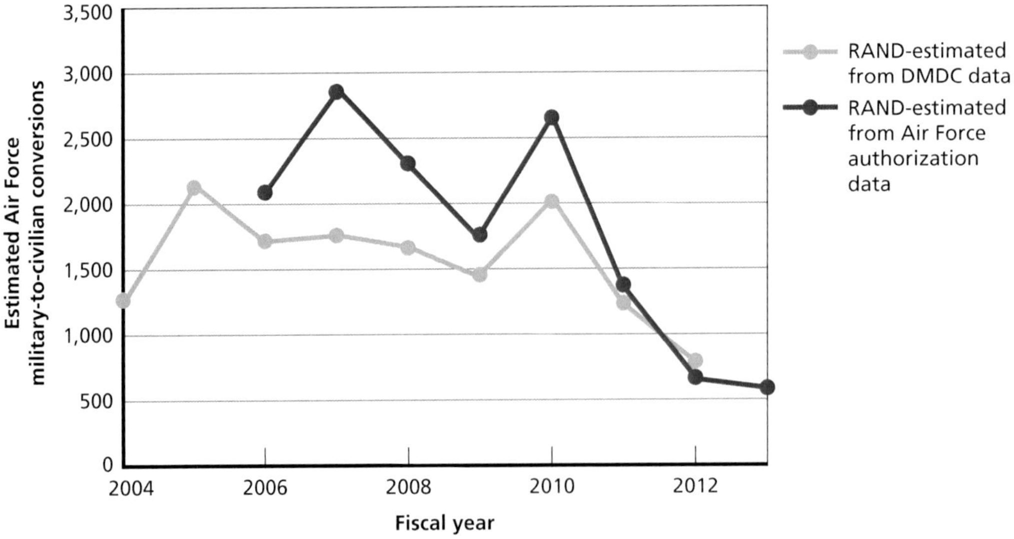

SOURCES: RAND-developed methodology using DMDC Military and Civilian Personnel Inventories and Air Force authorization data.
RAND *RR1282-3.11*

We found a greater discrepancy between DMDC data and estimates of military-to-civilian conversions provided in an OSD tabulation of cumulative military-to-civilian conversions by military service between FY 2004 and FY 2010.[9] These data are presented in Table 3.5.

As shown in Figure 3.12, our estimates of FYs 2004–2010 military-to-civilian conversions are quite different from OSD's. While we estimated somewhat more Air Force military-to-civilian conversions than the 2009 OSD estimates did, we estimated considerably fewer Army, Marine Corps, and, especially, Navy military-to-civilian conversions.

Our discussions with subject matter experts identified two possible explanations for the results in Figure 3.12. One Navy expert suggested that the Navy counted and reported conversions to OSD based on gross changes in workforce mix without any matching on occupation or locality. Hence, a Navy-calculated conversion could involve exchanging military authorizations in one function for civilian authorizations in a completely different function and possibly different location. The RAND algorithm would not identify such a Navy force reshaping as a conversion unless there were a match on both zip code and DoD occupation code. Another subject matter expert referred to "mils-to-nils," a shorthand for a military position being vacated and either not filled at all or performed by contractors. OSD may be counting these mils-to-nils as conversions; however, our algorithm would not identify them as such.

Table 3.5
OSD-Provided FYs 2004–2010 Cumulative Military-to-Civilian Conversions (Number of Military Personnel Converted)

Component	FY 2008	FY 2009	FY 2010
Air Force	8,240	8,875	10,070
Army	14,523	14,662	14,690
Marine Corps	3,811	4,111	4,436
Navy	15,682	17,258	19,110
Total	42,256	44,906	48,306

SOURCE: OSD, 2009, p. 165.

NOTE: The data shown for FYs 2008–2010 are cumulative totals of conversions that start at FY 2004. OSD, 2009, did not contain year-by-year breakdowns for FYs 2004–2007.

[9] CBO (2013) noted the conversion of 48,000 military positions to provision by 32,000 government-employed civilians between 2004 and 2010. When we queried CBO about the provenance of that estimate, they pointed us toward the tabulation presented in OSD, 2009, p. 165.

Figure 3.12
Comparing RAND and OSD Estimates of FYs 2004–2010 Military-to-Civilian Conversions

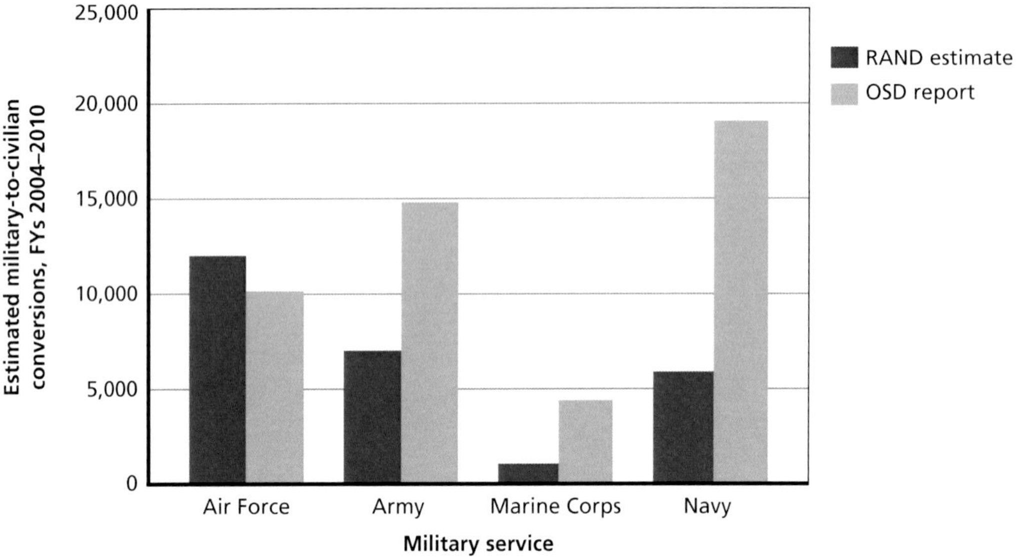

SOURCES: RAND-developed methodology using DMDC Military and Civilian Personnel Inventories and OSD, 2009, p. 165.

Summary

Our assessment of past experience with military-to-civilian conversion revealed that almost half of military personnel vacated their positions every year. This circumstance creates ongoing opportunities for responsibilities to be turned over to civilians, if so desired. In contrast, there is less turnover among government civilian personnel. On average, 17 percent of civilian personnel (about one in six) vacated their positions every year. These results provide evidence in support of the claim that civilian personnel provide more continuity than military personnel and reduce training needs.

Our RAND-developed conversion estimation technique found that both the number of converted positions and the number of occupations that experienced conversions varied greatly across the services. Our estimates found that almost three-fourths of September 30, 2012, Air Force military personnel worked in occupations in which the Air Force had military-to-civilian conversions over the time period FYs 2004–2012. In contrast, about half of September 30, 2012, Army military personnel worked in occupations in which the Army had military-to-civilian conversions over the FYs 2004–2012 period.

Over the same time frame, the services achieved military-to-civilian conversion substitution ratios averaging 70.7 percent—i.e., on average, approximately seven government civilians moved into positions that were previously held by ten military service members. This figure roughly aligns with a 2013 report by CBO that discussed the option of converting 70,000 positions from military to civilian provision over four years at a ratio of approximately two government civilians for every three military service members.[10] The substitution ratios that we estimated varied across the services and over time, ranging from 56.8 percent to 88.5 percent.

Military-to-civilian conversions are the exception rather than the norm. Very few positions vacated by military personnel are converted to civilian positions. Most are simply filled by other military members. The vast majority of military positions that are vacated and not filled by other military service members simply remain vacant. Our analysis did not reveal whether the underlying authorizations still existed.

When examining individual occupations, some experienced no conversions—not surprisingly, such combat-oriented occupations as Missile Guidance and Control (code 1121) and Aircraft Launch Equipment (code 1604) fall into this category. Others, most notably Security Guards (code 1070), experienced so many conversions that they are now filled entirely by civilian personnel. Most occupations exhibited some conversions, yet for the vast majority of these, military personnel still dominate the workforce. These occupation categories may provide opportunities for additional conversions.

---

[10] CBO, 2013.

CHAPTER FOUR

Impediments to Authorizing and Executing Military-to-Civilian Conversions

Our estimates of military-to-civilian conversions discussed in the previous chapter showed that such conversions are uncommon relative to the ongoing, large-scale turnover in military positions. Why is this the case? What impediments stand in the way of making greater use of this workforce shaping mechanism? The RAND team turned to human resources, manpower, and budget experts across DoD who had direct experience with military-to-civilian conversions to gain a better understanding of how the process works and the challenges involved.

Methodology

The RAND research team employed a qualitatively based expert elicitation method to identify the relevant subject matter experts with whom we spoke and to extract insights from those discussions. Aiming for a broad cross section across the services, we reached out to 29 individuals across the Air Force, Army, Marine Corps, Navy, and OSD, placing equal emphasis on each of the five components. Seventeen individuals responded to our request, allowing us to conduct 21 semi-structured discussions, each of which lasted approximately one hour.[1] Subject matter experts came from a variety of offices, including United States Navy Manpower and Readiness; United States Air Force Manpower and Readiness; United States Marine Corps Manpower and Reserve Affairs; and United States Army Special Operations Command, Force Management Division. Their backgrounds included direct experience with the A-76 process during the 1990s, working in OSD's Office of Cost Assessment and Program Evaluation (CAPE), and being closely involved in the Defense Agency Manpower Review Process. Appendix B provides details on the nature of the questions asked and the distribution of the subject matter experts across the components.

[1] We spoke with some respondents numerous times in order to clarify information provided in the initial discussion or solicit more detailed information on specific topics.

Process for Converting Positions from Military to Civilian Provision

We asked the subject matter experts to detail the process by which military positions were converted to government civilian positions. We bracketed the discussion by asking about the specific factors that precipitated the decision to convert positions, the procedural steps that followed, and the process by which converted positions were subsequently programmed and budgeted. Respondents also discussed how military-to-civilian conversions could be programmed and budgeted but, for a variety of reasons, might fail to be executed.

Circumstances That Precipitate Military-to-Civilian Conversions

Subject matter experts across the services reported that military-to-civilian conversions tend to occur for one of two reasons: (1) Military end strength is under pressure because of budget reductions, a drawdown, or a surge, or (2) cost savings are sought because of budget reductions or changes in spending priorities. One respondent also cited technological change as a factor that can precipitate military-to-civilian conversions.[2] However, most respondents identified pressure on military end strength and the need for cost savings as clear-cut catalysts for the decision to convert positions.

Many of the conversions that occurred over the FYs 2004–2010 period were precipitated by the surge in Iraq and Afghanistan. This was particularly true within the Army and Marine Corps. The surge required the services to move military personnel out of support positions to make them available for deployment. Converting those positions from military to civilian provision allowed the services to expand the pool of military personnel available for operational jobs while retaining the (now civilian) labor necessary to perform support functions.

Military end strength may also come under pressure as a result of budget reductions or a drawdown. While Congress or OSD may mandate the reduction in military personnel, the services generally have agency over which positions to cut and which to retain. If operation and maintenance (O&M) funds suffice, a service may elect to convert military positions to government civilian positions as an alternative to eliminating the military positions outright. Conversions permit the service to both comply with the mandated reduction in military personnel and maintain the labor required to perform critical functions.

Some of the conversions that occurred over the FYs 2004–2010 period were precipitated by a need to achieve cost savings. This was more true for the Navy and Air Force than for the Army and Marine Corps. Because government civilian person-

---

[2] In some cases, a change in technology may make it more cost-effective to have a civilian perform a function affected by the new technology. For instance, a technological advancement in an aircraft component may raise the cost of recruiting and training military personnel to repair that component. It may be less costly to hire civilians, who have been trained by the private sector, to perform the repairs. Such a circumstance could precipitate military-to-civilian conversions within the affected career fields.

nel are generally less costly than military personnel, implementing military-to-civilian conversions can generate cost savings, which can then be used to comply with budget reductions or to fund other needs. Four subject matter experts affiliated with the Navy reported that conversions were pursued in order to achieve cost savings. One of these described a number of conversions that were brought about by the Navy's Pay and Personnel Ashore (PAPA) initiative, which aimed to reduce the footprint afloat by moving two-thirds of personnel specialist billets ashore.[3] Many of these billets were converted to civilian positions so that the cost savings could be used to fund building renovations and other improvements.

Identifying Positions for Conversion from Military to Civilian Provision

Regardless of the catalyst, the next phase is to determine how many military positions will be converted, which positions will be converted, and when the conversions will occur. In some cases, these decisions are informed by an outside study. For instance, two respondents reported that the conversion of personnel specialist billets associated with the PAPA initiative was informed by an LMI report that recommended converting 2,000 positions over two years. In many cases, the general contours of these decisions are made by force planning and management staff within each service and are then pushed down to the relevant installations.

Installation commanders are asked to nominate military positions for conversion. In some cases, these requests are accompanied by specific targets (e.g., ten positions in each of the next four years) and/or specific occupations or grades within which the conversions should occur. In other cases, the nomination requests are more open-ended. In either case, subject matter experts suggested that the process by which installation commanders review military positions for possible conversion proceeds as represented by the following questions:

- **Is the position military essential?** If so, the position is not eligible for conversion. Considerations relating to military-unique knowledge, sea-to-shore rotation, career progression, and esprit de corps apply here.
- **For those positions that are not military essential, are there other reasons to have military personnel perform the functions?** For instance, does the position require long work hours? Is the position located in a remote area with few, if any, qualified civilian candidates? Are O&M funds insufficient to support employment of additional civilians?
- **For those positions that may be suitable for civilian provision, are the functions performed inherently governmental?** If so, the functions may not be per-

[3] See David M. Rodney, Michael D. Bowes, Christopher M. Duquette, and Sara M. Russell, with Kletus S. Lawler and Jessica S. Oi, *Impact of Manning and Infrastructure Initiatives on the Surface Navy*, Arlington, Va.: CNA, CRM D0021247.A2, 2009.

formed by a contractor. These positions are candidates for military-to-civilian conversion.

- **If the functions are not inherently governmental, are they better suited to a government civilian or a contractor?** Prior to the moratorium, an A-76 competition would have been administered to determine which would be more cost-effective. Those positions found to be better suited to civilian provision are candidates for conversion.

Nominations submitted by the installations are then reviewed by the relevant manpower and operations offices. The subject matter experts with whom we spoke indicated that within the Air Force, Army, and Navy, the relevant offices are the AF/A1M, the Office of the Deputy Chief of Staff for Operations and Plans (G-3), and OPNAV N1, respectively. The offices assess whether the nominated conversions adhere to the relevant guidelines, estimate the cost implications of converting the nominated positions, and evaluate the impact of the nominated conversions on the health of the force.

In some cases, the reviewing office does not approve one or more nominations. In other cases, the office requests that installations submit additional nominations. The office may elect to conduct its own billet-by-billet review in an effort to identify additional positions for conversion. Our respondents indicated that these billet-by-billet reviews focus more on the needs of the service as a whole than do the installation-level reviews and that cost considerations may play a more prominent role. Any additional positions identified are pushed down to the relevant installations. The installations may concede the conversions or offer arguments for preserving the positions as military billets. In any case, the reviewing office is the final arbiter.

Positions that are designated for conversion by the reviewing office are pushed up through the service hierarchy for additional review. For example, within the Navy, conversions approved by N1 are subject to review by N80, the Navy's programming division. The conversions are then submitted to the Chief of Naval Operations for approval and are ultimately reviewed by OSD.

Programming and Budgeting Military-to-Civilian Conversions

Subject matter experts across the services reported that the programming and budgeting processes are cumbersome and pose a number of challenges for military-to-civilian conversions. In this section, we provide a brief description of these processes, identify the features our respondents found to be most problematic, and discuss the implications of these features for military-to-civilian conversions.

Overview of the Programming and Budgeting Processes. The basic purpose of the programming process is to develop a five-year resource-allocation plan that reflects the department's objectives and capabilities. Each service develops its own plan, or

Program Objective Memorandum (POM), for submission to OSD. A new POM is developed and submitted every two years.

Competition over scarce resources is inherent in the POM process. For each appropriation, the resource office within the service sets a core funding level. The core identifies programs that do not require reevaluation during the POM cycle. Programs not covered by the core must compete for the remaining resources available within the service. Each service prioritizes and assigns relative values to the competing initiatives. The groups tasked with conducting these assessments are often organized by appropriation category. For instance, one group may review manpower initiatives while another reviews O&M initiatives and a third reviews military construction.[4] The service then consolidates the rankings developed by each group and constructs a complete POM for submission to OSD.

The basic purpose of the budgeting process is to translate the first two years of the POM into a Budget Estimate Submission (BES). One respondent explained, "Programming sets the broad parameters; budgeting gets to the detail of individual jobs." Each service develops its own BES for submission to OSD and OMB, who conduct a joint budget review.

The budgeting process features some of the same siloing exhibited by the programming process. Installations prepare budget estimates with supporting justification for submission to the relevant programs and resources office within the service. The analysts who review the submissions are organized by appropriation category. For instance, the analysts reviewing expenses that draw from the military personnel account are different from the analysts reviewing expenses that draw from the O&M account. The analysts adjust and consolidate the installation-level submissions to construct a single, detailed budget estimate for each appropriation. These are consolidated further by the service-level budget office and delivered concurrently to OSD and OMB.

Both the POM and BES are prepared and submitted two years in advance. So, for example, in 2004 the services proffered POM 2006, which covered FYs 2006–2011, and BES 2006, which covered FYs 2006 and 2007.

Implications for Military-to-Civilian Conversions. A majority of the subject matter experts with whom we spoke described gaps or disconnects inherent in the programming and budgeting processes that present challenges for converting positions from military to civilian provision. We discuss the three gaps mentioned most frequently and their impact on military-to-civilian conversions here.

Several respondents reported issues relating to the bifurcation between the military personnel and O&M accounts. Eliminating a military position requires a reduction in military personnel funding, while creating a civilian position requires an

[4] See Carl W. Miller, III, *The Programming and Budgeting Processes of the United States Marine Corps: An Investigation into Their Efficiency*, Monterey, Calif.: Naval Postgraduate School, thesis, 1999.

increase in O&M funding. In the words of one respondent, military-to-civilian conversions require "cutting one budget while asking for funds from another."

The subject matter experts described review processes that are siloed by appropriation, and a few asserted that coordination between analysts reviewing the military personnel budget and analysts reviewing the O&M budget is poor. One respondent stated, "The two chains do not communicate." This disconnect poses a risk at the installation level. Consider an installation that surrenders military billets while simultaneously requesting an increase in O&M funds to cover the cost of civilian replacements. The analysts reviewing military personnel expenditures may approve the reduction in billets, while the analysts reviewing O&M expenditures may deny the request for additional funds to guard against growth in the number of civilian personnel. When the O&M increase is denied, the installation must sacrifice either the civilian replacement, which could leave the installation shorthanded, or some other item covered by O&M funds.

Based on our discussions with subject matter experts, the programming and budgeting processes do not offer a mechanism by which installations can tie the surrender of a military position to an increase in O&M funds. However, it appears that such a link can be established at the OSD level. One respondent, who was involved with the 2008 Defense Agency Manpower Review Process, reported that funds were set aside to cover the cost of civilian replacements. "It was helpful to have money behind the conversion effort. . . . We stood up a civilian position for every conversion." Another respondent offered that setting funds aside may be necessary to garner support for conversions from the installations: "If you come in and are just competing in the POM, the odds are you won't successfully get extra [O&M funds] to support your replacement civilian manpower."

Another gap that was mentioned by subject matter experts is the one between funding for civilian personnel and civilian FTE ceilings. The hiring of new civilians to fill converted positions may be constrained by either factor. For instance, an installation may find itself unable to hire civilians despite the availability of O&M funds because the civilian FTE ceiling has been reached. One respondent described a situation in which "the FTE cap stopped hiring. . . . [You have] 650 positions that are funded but cannot be filled due to the FTE cap." Alternatively, an installation may find itself unable to hire civilians even when there is room beneath the civilian FTE ceiling because O&M funds are insufficient or are needed to fund another item. Another respondent noted that "authorizations provide FTEs, but sometimes there is not enough funding to fill the authorizations." Several respondents, but particularly those involved with military-to-civilian conversions at the installation level, cited these dual constraints as a source of frustration.

Finally, seven of the 15 subject matter experts with whom we spoke raised the challenges presented by the two years that elapse between the programming and budgeting process and the execution of authorized conversions. One respondent commented,

"You have to identify the billet in FY 2015, but the money has to be programmed in the POM for FY 2017 to make the conversion." The lag is problematic because several variables can and do change during the intervening two years, and these changes may reduce the relevance of the authorized plan.

For instance, suppose that DoD is planning for a surge. It may elect to both increase military authorizations and implement a number of military-to-civilian conversions in order to make more military personnel available for deployment. These plans might be reflected in the POM and BES as increases in military and civilian authorizations and increases in the military personnel and O&M accounts. Now suppose that within two years of the POM and BES submissions, conditions change such that the surge does not occur. The services are likely to find themselves with an excess supply of military personnel. Many of these service members will not deploy, and, as such, the services must place them in support positions—positions that had been slated for conversion to civilian provision. Consequently, the conversions are canceled, and the associated O&M funds are repurposed.

In the next section, we offer additional examples of conversions that were canceled or thwarted because of changes that occurred during the two years that elapsed between authorization and execution.

Executing Authorized Conversions

The execution of authorized conversions occurs at the installation level. During the two years that transpire between the authorization of the conversions (i.e., the POM and BES submissions) and the appropriation of funds that permit their execution, installations must plan for both the departure of the military personnel vacating the converted positions and the hiring and training of the civilians filling those positions.

On the military side, the installation must schedule the phasing out of the military position in accordance with the end of the vacating service member's current tour. As one respondent noted, the process can be challenging because "we [are] dealing with people's lives and personal situations." For example, the service member may request an extension to his or her current tour. Alternatively, the service member may elect to retire early. In either case, there may be some uncertainty about the exact timing of the service member's departure.

On the civilian side, the installation must plan for the hiring and training of the civilian replacement. The hiring process may not be initiated until the funds to support the new hire have been appropriated. In addition, two respondents indicated that the service member must vacate his or her position before the civilian hiring process can begin; however, we were not able to identify any policy that imposes such a restriction. In concert with the local human resources office, the installation prepares a position description, and the position is subsequently advertised. Applicants must then be screened, interviewed, hired, and trained.

Both the phasing out of military positions and the hiring of civilian replacements are vulnerable to complicating factors and uncertainty. However, the subject matter experts with whom we spoke generally agreed that it is easier to vacate military positions than it is to identify and hire suitable civilian replacements. In particular, the sluggishness and rigidity of the civilian hiring process were frequently cited as an impediment to filling positions in a timely fashion. One respondent reported, "It takes the Marine Corps 148 days to get someone new into the position, whereas the DoD standard is 90 days." Another respondent expressed frustration with the rule set that applies to civilian hiring, stating that the system "is not flexible enough to accommodate rapid civilian hires." The respondent offered preferences for veterans as an example of a requirement that complicates and slows the hiring process.

A few subject matter experts reported that the sluggishness of the civilian hiring process worsens in cases in which a large number of civilians must be hired at one time. In these cases, installations may experience persistent vacancies or meaningful gaps between the service member's departure and the civilian replacement's arrival. Hiring gap contractors may be necessary. Even when the hiring process is speedy enough to close the gap between military departure and civilian arrival, the installation may experience a capabilities gap as the new civilians are trained and learn how to perform their functions.

As noted earlier, there is a two-year lag between the time when conversions are programmed and budgeted and the time when conversions are executed. During those two years, conditions may change such that executing the authorized conversions is no longer feasible. One respondent cited sequestration as an example of such a change in circumstance. When sequestration results in civilian furloughs or hiring freezes, it is simply not possible to acquire civilian replacements. Another factor that is subject to change over a two-year period is the availability of qualified civilians in the local labor market. Several respondents spoke of cases in which a service member rotated out of a converted position, but the installation was not able to subsequently identify a suitable civilian replacement.

When authorized conversions are not executed as planned such that positions slated for conversion and vacated by military personnel are left unfilled, installations may find themselves shorthanded. In some cases, the work is not performed. In other cases, the work is distributed among the existing or remaining workforce (both military and civilian) or performed by contractors who are brought in to cover the labor shortage.

Therefore, authorizing conversions is not sufficient. Failure to execute planned conversions may result in forfeiture of the cost savings that the conversions were intended to generate. If the workload shouldered by the outgoing service member is not transferred to a newly hired government civilian but instead is covered by a more expensive contractor or the overtime hours of existing civilian personnel, then costs may increase rather than decrease.

For this reason, it is important to consider not only the factors that impede the authorization of military-to-civilian conversions but also the factors that impede the execution of authorized conversions. Among the impediments discussed in the following section, some apply to the authorization of conversions, others to their execution, and a few impact both the authorization and execution of military-to-civilian conversions.

Impediments to Military-to-Civilian Conversions

Our conversations with subject matter experts revealed a number of perceived impediments to more effective use of military-to-civilian conversions as a tool to shape the DoD workforce. In this section, we present the five most salient impediments that emerged from these discussions: (1) Civilian positions are more vulnerable to cuts than military positions are, (2) some military positions are inappropriately shielded from conversion, (3) local commanders perceive military personnel to be free from cost, (4) civilian candidates may not be available to fill the converted positions, and (5) practical guidance on the process for executing authorized conversions is sparse.

Civilian Positions Are More Vulnerable to Cuts Than Military Positions Are

Our subject matter experts perceive civilian positions to be more vulnerable to cuts than military positions are. As noted earlier in the chapter, civilian hiring is subject to dual constraints: civilian FTE ceilings and O&M funds. Either constraint may bind. Hiring freezes precipitated by sequestration or other budget-related issues further constrain the hiring of civilians to fill converted positions.

Several respondents reported that installations cannot tie the surrender of a military position to increases in civilian authorizations or O&M funds. As such, proposing military-to-civilian conversions exposes installations to the risk of losing military personnel without securing the means to hire new civilians. There is some precedent for OSD setting funds aside to cover civilian replacements. However, three respondents suggested that doing so is politically unpalatable. Said one, "The optics of growing civilian positions while you draw down military positions are bad."

Four subject matter experts suggested that the relative vulnerability of civilian positions incentivizes commanders to guard against civilianization. "A lot of folks were worried that if they converted, they would not be able to keep the civilian billets," said one. Commanders are primarily concerned with having sufficient personnel to cover the workloads at their installations. As such, they may elect not to identify positions for conversion in order to preserve the size of the workforce. In this way, the relative vulnerability of civilian positions impedes not only the execution of conversions but also their authorization.

Recent events have magnified the perception that civilian positions are less protected than military positions. In 2013, federal government employees were furloughed twice. Almost all of the DoD civilian workforce was furloughed in March of that year as a result of budget sequestration. "Non-essential" government employees were furloughed in October due to a federal government shutdown. Military personnel, however, were not directly affected. The president exempted military personnel accounts from sequestration in FY 2013, and active-duty military personnel were paid during the shutdown.

Forthcoming congressional action may make civilian positions even more vulnerable to cuts. In January 2015, U.S. Representative Ken Calvert introduced H.R. 340, the Rebalance for an Effective Defense Uniformed and Civilian Employees (REDUCE) Act, to the House Committee on Armed Services. The bill calls for a 15-percent reduction in the defense civilian workforce over the next five years. Rep. Calvert has stated:

> The growth of the civilian workforce within the DoD continues to create a significant budgetary burden but, more importantly, if left unchecked it will negatively impact our men and women in uniform. Many of our civilians at the Pentagon and around the world do a fine job but their growth is unsustainable.[5]

In March 2015, Defense Secretary Ashton Carter told Congress that "civilian workforce reductions need to be part of the Pentagon's strategy to deal with tightening budgets. . . . [A]lthough parts of the workforce have grown out of necessity over the last decade, the Pentagon has not done enough to reduce overhead in its civilian ranks."[6]

That same month, *The Hill* published an article titled "Pentagon Should Cut Civilian, Not Military, Personnel." The piece argued that "enormous civilian employment is difficult to reconcile with [DoD's] stated mission" and called for more creativity in "how uniformed personnel might serve the department in new and more efficient ways than the existing legion of civilians on the payroll."[7]

Whether civilian positions are, in reality, more vulnerable to cuts than military positions are is immaterial. The perception suffices to discourage commanders from identifying positions for conversion.

Some Military Positions Are Inappropriately Shielded from Conversion

Not all positions can or should be converted to civilian positions. Our discussions with subject matter experts indicated that many protected positions are appropriately categorized as such. As discussed in Chapter Two, some positions that are classified as

---

[5] Eric Katz, "Republican Lawmakers Want to Cut 115,000 Civilian Defense Jobs," *Government Executive*, March 17, 2014.

[6] Jared Serbu, "Carter Opens Door to More DoD Civilian Job Cuts," Federal News Radio, March 5, 2015.

[7] Timothy Wilson, "Pentagon Should Cut Civilian, Not Military, Personnel," *The Hill*, April 3, 2014.

military essential, such as infantry and fighter pilots, cannot be converted—nor should they be.

Other positions that perhaps should be considered for civilian provision are protected as a matter of policy. 10 U.S.C. 129(c) hinders the services from reducing the number of uniformed military in medical positions and prohibits the services from converting medical and dental positions.[8] Four of our subject matter experts described such restrictions as counterproductive. One individual asserted that there was ample opportunity for conversion of medical positions in the Navy. Another stated that, prior to the prohibition instituted by the FY 2008 NDAA, conversions in the Navy medical community were more common. During this period, the entire medical community—including military and civilian practitioners—would be considered when staffing stateside hospitals in the wake of forward-deployed military departures. Yet another subject matter expert reported that one office requested 1,400 medical conversions in 2013 but received approval for only 180.

Still other positions are shielded from civilian provision for reasons of culture and/or tradition. Our subject matter experts suggested that entrenched cultural norms and traditions within the military complicate the civilianization of certain positions, such as recruiting and entry control point positions. They described a prevailing "comfort level" that results from seeing such jobs performed by uniformed service members. A few respondents suggested that commanders may prefer military personnel because they obey commands and can work long hours without overtime pay.

Ambiguities in policy facilitate the protection of such positions. Installations may appeal to such considerations as esprit de corps, career development, or sea-to-shore rotation to justify the preservation of particular military positions. For instance, a commander could argue that a particular position, which may not be classified as military essential in the first order, should be reserved for military provision because the position serves to prepare military service members for positions further up the chain that more clearly qualify as military essential. The relevant manpower or operations office within the service reviews the arguments and makes the final call. However, there is room for the office to exercise subjective judgment in doing so. A few subject matter experts suggested that subjectivity in making these determinations may enable the protection of some positions that should be civilianized.

Local Commanders Perceive Military Personnel to Be Free from Cost

Another factor that may affect military-to-civilian conversions is commanders' perceptions of the relative cost of military personnel. Military personnel appropriations funding is a central account budgeted at the service level rather than the installation

---

[8] 10 U.S.C. 129(c), *Medical Personnel: Limitations on Reductions*, amended by Public Law 111-84, *National Defense Authorization Act for Fiscal Year 2010*, Section 701, October 28, 2009, and Public Law 110-181, *National Defense Authorization Act for Fiscal Year 2008*, Section 721, January 28, 2008.

level. In contrast, O&M funding, which covers the cost of civilian personnel and contracts for services, as well as a number of other items, is managed at the installation level. Consequently, commanders internalize the trade-offs between civilian personnel, contractors, and other items paid from the O&M account. Because military personnel are covered by a separate, centrally managed account, commanders do not internalize the trade-offs between military personnel and civilian personnel in the same fashion.

Of the 15 subject matter experts with whom we spoke, four argued that the funding distinction causes installations to treat military personnel as "free" relative to civilian personnel, providing an incentive for commanders to obstruct military-to-civilian conversions. One respondent noted, "The incentive is to keep as much military as you can. If there is a function you want to get, your first try is to use military personnel to do it because they are free."

The issue is exacerbated by installations' inability to link the surrender of a military position to increases in civilian authorizations or O&M funds. If installations were able to "cash in" a military position in exchange for the means to hire a new civilian, the price of military personnel would, in effect, be set equal to the forgone O&M funds, and local commanders would internalize the trade-off between military and civilian personnel. Unfortunately, the siloing inherent in current programming and budgeting processes stymies the establishment of such a link, causing local commanders to regard military personnel as free from cost.

Several subject matter experts mentioned incentive problems or distortions rooted in the siloed approach to programming and budgeting. One respondent affiliated with the Navy offered that "commanders do want to experience the savings [associated with military-to-civilian conversions], but the savings are captured by the 'big Navy' to pay for something else." Another respondent affiliated with the Army noted that "the pots of money are a problem. . . . [W]e end up managing the civilian FTE and not by dollars."

Despite the costs incurred at the installation level, commanders may prefer civilian personnel for a number of reasons. Commanders can exercise more control over filling civilian positions than they can over manning military positions. Unmanned military positions are quite common. Commanders can keep civilian positions filled at a higher rate if they elect to do so. In addition, commanders have greater agency in selecting the individuals filling civilian positions than they have in selecting the individuals occupying military positions. These advantages may induce commanders to convert positions from military to civilian provision in spite of the draw on O&M funds.

A related issue arises from the difference between cost to DoD and cost to the federal government as a whole. Active-duty service members cost less to DoD because a significant portion of their costs is borne by other federal agencies, such as the Department of Veterans Affairs, the Department of the Treasury, the Office of Personnel Management, and the Department of Education. In contrast, civilian personnel cost more to DoD because few of their costs are borne by other federal agencies and because their higher taxable incomes, while generating larger tax payments to the Treasury, do not count as offsetting receipts to DoD.[9]

A recent CBO report found that, on average, a civilian occupying a DoD commercial position costs the federal government as a whole 29 percent less than an active-duty service member in a similar position: about $96,000 per year compared with $135,200. However, the civilian costs DoD 3 percent *more* than the comparable active-duty service member: about $106,100 per year compared with $103,400.[10]

None of the subject matter experts with whom we spoke mentioned differences between costs borne by DoD and costs borne by the federal government as a whole. Nevertheless, one can reasonably conclude from the figures provided by CBO that DoD's incentive to convert positions from military to civilian provision is weakened by the fact that other federal agencies cover a meaningful share of the cost of military personnel.

Civilian Candidates May Not Be Available to Fill the Converted Positions

Well-qualified civilians must be available in the surrounding area and must be willing to assume the challenges and responsibilities required of a converted position. Our subject matter experts reported that, in some cases, conversions are authorized but not executed because of a lack of qualified civilians in the local labor market. Significant lags between the authorization of conversions and the search for suitable civilian candidates appear to raise the likelihood that converted positions will remain vacant. In addition to possessing the requisite qualifications, civilians must be willing to accept the challenges and rigors of the new position, which may include adjusting to the norms, rules, and expectations of military work. Moreover, new civilian hires must be satisfied with the pay or salary offered by the government.

Qualified Civilians. After a position is authorized for conversion, a well-qualified and appropriately skilled civilian candidate must fill it. Several subject matter experts intimated that this can be harder than it seems; one respondent described the unavailability of qualified civilians as the largest impediment to executing conversions. Identifying a suitable civilian candidate is particularly challenging when the position is located in a remote area or requires special skills. Civilian neurosurgeons, for example, are unlikely to seek employment in rural areas.

Planning helps, but problems can still arise. An advance analysis of the local labor market can provide an estimate of the prevalence of civilians with the requisite qualifications and competencies. However, in many cases the estimate is merely a snapshot; people and their circumstances are ever-changing, and a skilled civilian labor pool that exists one month may be gone or depleted the next. The two-year lag between the time

---

9 CBO, 2015.

10 CBO, 2015.

when conversions are programmed and budgeted and the time when conversions are executed mitigates the relevance of the labor market analysis and magnifies the risk of failing to hire suitable civilian replacements. One subject matter expert described such an instance: "The initial market analysis showed [that] we had folks in the area with those skills, but when we went to get them, they were not there."

The sluggishness and rigidity of the civilian hiring process were frequently cited as aggravating factors. The hiring process may not be initiated until the funds to support the new civilian hire have been appropriated. From that point, it may take three to six months to fill the position. A few subject matter experts reported that delays worsen in cases where a large number of civilians must be hired at one time.

Willing Civilians. In addition to possessing the requisite qualifications, civilian candidates who fill military positions must be willing to adjust to the norms, rules, and expectations of a military work environment. Some civilian candidates have prior military experience; however, this is not the case in every locality or for every occupation. Civilian hires who lack exposure to military personnel and processes must be willing to integrate into the military setting and perform satisfactorily despite cultural newness and steep learning curves.

A few subject matter experts mentioned that some newly hired civilian employees are dissatisfied with the pay or salary that accompanies government positions. If the dissatisfaction reduces retention rates, then the cost benefits of replacing military personnel with civilian personnel may not materialize. Our discussions suggest that dissatisfaction with pay or salary is more likely to occur when the civilians hired have no prior experience in the military or civil service.

Identifying and hiring suitable civilians can be a challenging task. The individuals stepping into the converted positions must be both qualified to perform the work and willing to operate in a military environment at a government wage. Civilian candidates who meet these criteria are not available in every locality or for every occupation. Advance analysis of the local labor market and prompt execution of authorized conversions can reduce, but not eliminate, the risk of ending up with vacant positions—and a smaller workforce overall.

Practical Guidance on the Process for Executing Authorized Conversions Is Sparse

Existing policies provide abundant guidance on the criteria used to identify positions for conversion and the process for programming and budgeting the conversions identified. However, guidance on the process for executing authorized conversions is sparse.

Considerations relating to the determination of an appropriate workforce mix and the identification of positions for military-to-civilian conversion are well covered by a range of statutes, directives, and instructions, as described in Chapter Two. Existing doctrine addresses the criteria that qualify a position as military essential, as well as the role of mission effectiveness and cost in determining the appropriate mix of military service members, government civilian personnel, and contracts for services.

Programming and budgeting processes are also well understood and documented, as described earlier in this chapter and in Chapter Two.

Less attention is paid to the process for *executing* conversions. Subject matter experts expressed confusion about the process, which is necessarily complicated because it involves synchronizing military assignments with the civilian hiring process. For instance, two respondents indicated that the civilian hiring process cannot begin until the military position has been vacated. However, we were not able to identify any policy that precludes installations from hiring a civilian replacement prior to the service member's departure.

The subject matter experts opined that confusion over what the process for executing conversions is and how to navigate it can exacerbate what are already lengthy delays between authorization and execution. These delays, in turn, can impede the execution of conversions in a number of ways. For instance, suitable civilian candidates may no longer be available in the relevant locality.

Most subject matter experts reported that they were not aware of any policy documents or guidance relating to the process for executing military-to-civilian conversions. One respondent associated with the Navy stated, "A lot of the problem was that there [were] not a lot of good documented policies and no good written guidance on how to execute conversions." This respondent reported reaching out to the other services for guidance: "We coordinated to learn from them."

Clearly written, practical guidance on the process for executing military-to-civilian conversions could reduce the confusion described by subject matter experts. The tangible benefit would likely be a reduction in the lag time between authorizations and execution, which would reduce the frequency of failed executions. The guidance could be developed by either the department or the services; we are agnostic on this point. The objective is simply to provide practitioners with a clear path from authorization to execution.

Enthusiasm Remains for Military-to-Civilian Conversions

Our subject matter experts expressed frustration with the various impediments mentioned throughout this chapter. However, the presence of impediments to the conversion process does not negate the prospective benefits of civilian personnel. There is, in fact, a very discernable silver lining. While a few subject matter experts opined that military service members prefer to interact with other military personnel, most of our experts voiced general support for an increased role for civilians in DoD.

One expert noted, "Commanders like having civilians in the workspace. There are great advantages. They don't deploy or require ancillary training. It's a great value, and you get a more efficient organization."[11] Another noted that civilian conversions "allowed us to retain true experts in our program. Many civilians come from the civil service and bring a lot of experience with them. Continuity and expertise is what you get. Seventy percent of my civilians are former military, so they have a lot of institutional knowledge. The continuity piece is important."

Even more encouraging is the realization that every impediment identified during our expert elicitation exercise pertained to the conversion *process* and not to the civilian employees themselves. Many of the process-oriented frustrations that were expressed related to the ambiguity and disorganization of conversions. One respondent stated, "There are performance benefits to conversions, but the implementation is painful."

The most significant concern cited by the subject matter experts was the ability to secure sufficient personnel to cover the workload, regardless of the mix of military service members, government civilian personnel, and contracts for services. Military-to-civilian conversions that led to a reduction in the total number of available personnel with no commensurate reduction in workload were met with less enthusiasm. Where military personnel were replaced with civilian personnel at a one-for-one rate, subject matter experts reported more positive experiences, more support for military-to-civilian conversions, and more visibility of the value that civilian employees can bring to the workplace.

It is worth noting that the conversions that occurred during the FYs 2004–2010 period were, in many cases, designed to make military personnel available for deployment. These conversions were not accompanied by a reduction in military end strength. Support for conversions in the services or OSD may waiver in the future if conversions are driven by a cost-savings initiative that results in cuts to military personnel or to the DoD workforce across the board.

Summary

A question of particular interest to DoD is why so few military-to-civilian conversions are undertaken—what impediments stand in the way. Our discussions with subject matter experts across DoD revealed that impediments to military-to-civilian conversions affect both the authorization and execution of conversions. For this reason, efforts

---

[11] Another respondent spoke at length about the efficiency improvements that followed the conversions brought about by the Navy's PAPA initiative. The conversion of over 2,000 personnel specialist billets was programmed and budgeted such that only 70 percent of the reduction in the military pay accounts was converted to an increase in O&M funding. The remaining 30 percent was set aside for building renovations and other improvements. The new civilians that were hired were quite a bit more efficient. When the positions were staffed by military personnel, the number of transactions processed per person per year was approximately 650. Following the conversions, the number rose dramatically. The current number of transactions processed per person per year is approximately 1500. That constitutes an efficiency improvement of 130 percent, which far exceeds the 43 percent efficiency improvement associated with replacing ten service members with seven civilians.

to improve the process need to consider both stages. The most salient impediments that emerged from our discussions are the following:

- Civilian positions are more vulnerable to cuts than military positions are.
- Some military positions are inappropriately shielded from conversion.
- Local commanders perceive military personnel to be free from cost.
- Civilian candidates may not be available to fill converted positions.
- Practical guidance on the process for executing authorized conversions is sparse.

Despite these impediments, most of the subject matter experts with whom we spoke voiced general support for an increased role for civilians in DoD. Military commanders value the experience and continuity that civilian personnel bring to the workplace. In addition, many DoD civilian employees have prior military experience and, as such, are accustomed to working in a military environment. Manpower analysts in the services and OSD recognize that, in most cases, civilian personnel cost less than military personnel or contractors. Many of them favor military-to-civilian conversions as a means of capturing cost savings.

CHAPTER FIVE

Recommendations

The RAND team investigated the topic of military-to-civilian conversions from three perspectives:

- a review of statutes and policies governing performance of work by military service members, government civilian employees, and contractors
- an analysis of the most recent experience with military-to-civilian conversions (FYs 2004–2012) using DMDC data
- discussions with human resources, manpower, and budget experts across DoD who had experience with military-to-civilian conversions.

Looking across these research threads, the RAND team identified a number of opportunities for Congress, OSD, and/or the services to improve statutes, policies, and business practices in order to facilitate military-to-civilian conversions and motivate greater use of this force management tool, should that be DoD's goal. The remainder of this chapter presents our recommendations, as well as some considerations for DoD, should a next wave of military-to-civilian conversions commence.

Changes to Statutes

Repeal the prohibition on converting medical and dental positions.

Section 701 of the FY 2010 NDAA prohibits the services from converting any medical or dental position from military to civilian provision.[1] The prohibition is without exception: The services may not convert medical or dental positions even if the conversions can be shown to reduce costs without compromising access to or quality of care. Several subject matter experts reported that there is ample opportunity for conversions of medical personnel but that very few such conversions are approved, as a consequence

[1] 10 U.S.C. 129(c), *Medical Personnel: Limitations on Reductions*, amended by Public Law 111-84, *National Defense Authorization Act for Fiscal Year 2010*, Section 701, October 28, 2009, and Public Law 110-181, *National Defense Authorization Act for Fiscal Year 2008*, Section 721, January 28, 2008.

of the statutory restriction. Repealing the prohibition—or, alternatively, amending the statute to permit cost-effective conversions[2]—would permit the services to staff medical and dental positions with the "most appropriate and cost efficient mix" of military and civilian personnel, as directed by 10 U.S.C. 129(a).

Amend Section 955 to exclude increases in civilian personnel funding that result from cost-effective military-to-civilian conversions.

Section 955 of the FY 2013 NDAA mandates reductions in civilian personnel and contractor expenditures that are commensurate with reductions in funding for basic military personnel pay achieved from reductions in military end strengths. The statute does provide for certain exceptions. For instance, expenses for civilian personnel employed in "Mission Critical Occupations" or at "facilities providing core logistics capabilities" are excluded from the mandated reductions.[3] However, these exclusions are insufficient: The statute provides no allowance for military-to-civilian conversions that raise civilian personnel expenditures but reduce the overall cost of personnel, military and civilian.

Changes to Policies

Relax the civilian FTE ceilings to exclude civilian positions arising from cost-effective military-to-civilian conversions.

Eight of the 15 subject matter experts with whom we spoke cited civilian FTE ceilings as a significant impediment to military-to-civilian conversions. One respondent described a situation in which 650 positions that were authorized for conversion—and funded—could not be filled because of the FTE cap. Moreover, the adverse effects of the civilian personnel caps may extend beyond failed executions of authorized conversions. Four subject matter experts suggested that commanders may be reluctant to identify positions for conversion to avoid losing the positions altogether once they are civilianized.

Relaxing the civilian FTE ceilings would facilitate the execution of authorized conversions and provide local commanders with appropriate incentives for identifying positions for conversion. As an alternative to lifting the civilian FTE ceilings across the board, OSD could offer exceptions that apply specifically to military-to-civilian conversions. For instance, the department could issue waivers from civilian personnel caps for civilian positions that arise from cost-effective conversions.

---

2 Amending Section 701 of the FY 2010 NDAA to permit cost-effective conversions could be achieved by reverting to the language of Section 742 of the FY 2007 NDAA (Public Law 109-364, *National Defense Authorization Act for Fiscal Year 2007*).

3 Public Law 112-239, *National Defense Authorization Act for Fiscal Year 2013*.

Develop clearer, more precise definitions for the military essential criteria.
Some military positions are inappropriately shielded from conversion to civilian provision for reasons of culture and/or tradition. Installations can argue that certain positions qualify as military essential by appealing to such considerations as esprit de corps, career development, or sea-to-shore rotation. These criteria leave room for interpretation, and, in some cases, subjectivity in determining whether these criteria apply has enabled the protection of military positions for reasons other than mission effectiveness and cost.

Eliminating such room for interpretation entirely is likely not possible—or desirable. Local commanders have a more detailed understanding of the specific workings of their installations and should be able to exercise some authority and judgment in managing their workforces. Nevertheless, OSD should explore ways to tighten the definitions of the military essential criteria. For example, the department might consider tying the career development and rotation criteria to appropriate metrics, which might vary by service.

Issue practical guidance addressing the process for executing authorized conversions.
Existing policies provide abundant guidance on the criteria used to identify positions for conversion and the process for programming and budgeting the conversions identified. However, practical guidance on the process for executing authorized conversions is sparse. The process is necessarily complicated because it involves synchronizing military assignments with the civilian hiring process. Reducing ambiguities and confusion surrounding the process may shorten the elapsed time between authorization and execution of conversions, increase the likelihood of executing conversions that have been authorized, and improve the experience of commanders and managers engaged in implementing conversions. Written guidance could be developed by DoD or by the services; we are agnostic on this point. The objective is to provide practitioners with a clear path from authorization to execution.

Develop a clear definition of military-to-civilian conversion and stipulate that data reporting across the services be consistent with that definition.
The data reveal a gap between authorized conversions and executed conversions. In some cases, the gap appears to be artificial—a consequence of inconsistent practices in the reporting of military-to-civilian conversions. One subject matter expert reported that the Navy's reporting of authorized conversions is based on a gross calculation of changes in the workforce mix without any matching on occupation or locality. This might explain the gap between our estimated conversions for the Navy and Marine Corps and the figures reported by OSD. Inconsistencies in measuring and reporting conversions impede effective tracking and analysis.

Changes to Business Practices

Amend the programming and budgeting processes to permit installations to tie the surrender of a military position to a compensating increase in O&M funds.
Our discussions revealed that service-level processes for reviewing proposed conversions are siloed by appropriation. A few respondents asserted that coordination between analysts reviewing the military personnel budget and analysts reviewing the O&M budget is poor. Consequently, proposing military-to-civilian conversions exposes installations to the risk of losing military personnel without securing the means to hire new civilians. Savings from converting positions are captured by the service but not by the installations, which perceive military personnel to be free from cost. There is some precedent for OSD setting funds aside to cover civilian replacements, but doing so in the current environment appears to be politically unpalatable.

In order to better align the incentives of the installation with the incentives of the service as a whole, the programming and budgeting processes should be amended to permit installations to tie the surrender of a military position to a compensating increase in O&M funds. Strengthening the link between the two funding lines at the installation level would allow the installations to capture the cost savings associated with military-to-civilian conversions. If installations were able to "cash in" a military position in exchange for the means to hire a new civilian, the price of military personnel would, in effect, be set equal to the forgone O&M funds, and the installation would internalize the trade-off between military and civilian personnel.

A soft approach to strengthening the link might include instituting practices that improve coordination among reviewing analysts across appropriation categories. A more direct approach might include establishing a requirement that the installation's O&M budget rise by an amount commensurate to the cost of the surrendered military position.

Reduce the time between authorization and execution of conversions.
In order to raise the likelihood that authorized conversions are realized, the services must shorten the time that elapses between authorization and execution. Our discussions with subject matter experts indicated that the culprits include the following:

- the two-year lag between the time when conversions are programmed and budgeted and the time when funds are appropriated
- the sluggishness and rigidity of the civilian hiring process
- general confusion about the process for executing authorized conversions.

Commanders and managers need a clear and viable plan for navigating and synchronizing the military and civilian personnel systems. Process improvements addressing the root causes enumerated above may be driven by written guidance, changes to business practices, or both.

Conduct an assessment of the local market for civilian labor before authorizing conversions.

One way to increase the likelihood of executing conversions that have been authorized is to conduct due diligence prior to authorization. In particular, an assessment of the local market for civilian labor should precede authorization of military-to-civilian conversions. The assessment should provide information about the availability of qualified and willing candidates for the civilian positions that will become available and account for the two-year lag between the time when conversions are programmed and budgeted and the time when funds are appropriated. Excessive delays between authorization and execution should be avoided so that the conversions can be executed before market conditions change. Our discussions with subject matter experts indicated that these assessments are frequently conducted, but not always, and, in some cases, the quality of the assessment is poor.

Leverage personnel data to identify occupations or installations that could yield additional conversions.

OSD and/or the services could leverage personnel data to identify occupations or installations that may yield additional conversions. Analysis of personnel data may be able to provide answers to a number of relevant questions, including the following:

- Which occupations have experienced conversions in the recent past?
- Have the civilians who stepped into these converted positions been retained? Have they been promoted?
- Are there additional military personnel in these occupations that could also be replaced with civilian personnel?
- Which occupations have not experienced conversions?
- Are there discernible reasons that explain why conversions have not occurred in these occupations? (For example, is the occupation clearly military essential?)
- Are these reasons consistent with statutes, instructions, and guidance?
- Are there occupations in which conversions are prevalent for one service but not for another service?

Improve and standardize data collection on contracts for services.

A limitation of the data analysis we conducted is that the data set covered military and government civilian personnel only; comparable data for contractors were not available. As a result, our analysis does not speak to conversions into or out of contractor provision. Moreover, while the data analysis reveals a gap between *authorized* conversions (reported by OSD or estimated by the RAND team using Air Force data) and *executed* conversions (estimated by the RAND team using DMDC data), the analysis does not provide information on whether the observed gap was filled using contractors. If a support contract replaced a vacated military position, the DMDC data would not see the contractor, and our algorithm would, therefore, not identify that a conversion had occurred. The only indication we have of such a phenomenon consists of reports from the subject matter experts with whom we spoke. Improved and standardized data collection on contractors would facilitate these and other analyses of workforce mix.

Looking Ahead

Ensure that estimates of the cost savings associated with military-to-civilian conversions reflect substitution ratios that are feasible in practice.

As discussed earlier, a 2013 CBO report presented the option of converting 70,000 positions from military to civilian provision over four years at a ratio of approximately two government civilians for every three military service members. CBO estimated that these replacements "could reduce the need for appropriations by $20 billion and for discretionary outlays by $19 billion from 2015 through 2023."[4]

The cost savings projected by CBO depend on the feasibility of implementing the two-for-three substitution ratio. Our analysis of DMDC data suggests that the ratio can be implemented. On average, across the four services and over the FYs 2004–2012 period, the estimated ratio of civilians filling positions vacated and not filled by military service members was 70.7 percent—just short of the ratio examined by CBO.

However, our discussions with subject matter experts suggest that implementing such a ratio may not be feasible in every case. The 2:3 ratio is more easily implemented when there are large numbers of similar conversions (same installation and occupation) occurring simultaneously. When only one or two similar conversions occur at a time, implementation of the 2:3 ratio is simply not possible.

DoD, CBO, and other organizations engaged in forecasting the cost savings associated with military-to-civilian conversions should account for such practical realities when developing their estimates.

Plan for increased resistance to conversions if the conversions are designed to reduce military end strength.

Military-to-civilian conversions that occurred between FY 2004 and FY 2010 were designed to make military personnel available for deployment. If the next wave of conversions is designed to reduce military end strength instead (as discussed by CBO), then OSD should plan for increased resistance by the services. Stronger guidance—perhaps in the form of targets for military-to-civilian conversions—may be necessary. Analysis of personnel data could be used to inform such guidance.

---

4 CBO, 2013.

APPENDIX A

Best Practices for Employing Military-to-Civilian Conversions

As the previous chapters have shown, military-to-civilian conversions are not the norm, and the ability to execute such conversions is replete with challenges. There are personnel limitations imposed by statutes and guidance to be navigated. There are challenges associated with identifying positions, gaining authorizations, and executing conversions. There are even differences of opinion about what level of savings can be achieved—largely associated with execution and economies of scale. So, given these challenges, is it possible to identify a set of best practices that could guide DoD in the future?

To answer this question, the RAND team turned to the research literature. We searched a number of scholarly databases, including WorldCat, Web of Science, and JSTOR, as well as more specialized defense-related resources: DTIC (Defense Technical Information Center) Online and the Air University Library Index to Military Periodicals. Search terms included the following words and phrases: military civilian conversion, civilianization, insourcing, cost/pay of military and civilian personnel/employees, defense/DoD workforce mix/composition, workforce planning/assessment, A-76 cost comparison, and defense/DoD human capital management. In addition, we searched the databases of institutions that work on these topics: the U.S. Government Accountability Office (GAO; known as the U.S. General Accounting Office until 2004), CBO, the Congressional Research Service, the RAND Corporation, the Institute for Defense Analyses (IDA), and CNA Corporation. Finally, we searched for relevant academic theses by graduates of the military academies and the Naval Postgraduate School. While there have been important contributions from other sources, GAO and RAND are responsible for the bulk of the research conducted in this area.

We restricted our search to English-language, U.S. publications but did not restrict the time frame. Although the vast majority of the literature we reviewed was published after 2000, we included some key early studies, including GAO reports from 1969 and 1972 noting the extensive use of military personnel in civilian roles, GAO reports from 1978 and 1982 recommending the civilianization of certain military support positions, and RAND reports from 1988 and 1998 comparing the costs of military and civilian employees.[1]

Ultimately, we reviewed over 100 documents from this rich literature base and identified 75 that were particularly relevant to our study. We focused on studies that offered lessons from past experiences with military-to-civilian conversions and could inform a set of best practices for successfully executing such conversions in the future.

A striking feature of these studies is the consistency of the findings and recommendations and the persistence of the key challenges identified. For example, as early as 1969, GAO noted in a study of the Coast Guard that there was a "large number of civilian-type positions . . . occupied by military personnel" and that there were "substantial savings attainable by civilianization." Furthermore, the 1969 report notes that "restrictions on civilian employment" made military leaders reluctant to support conversions because of fears that "future conversion will result not only in the loss of military billets but also in the abolishment of an appreciable number of the replacement civilian positions." The report states further that prior conversions were conducted on an ad hoc basis, and not as part of a continuing program, and found no evidence of effective action to implement the government's general policy that civilian-type positions be filled by civilian personnel. The report concludes that the issue should be brought to Congress's attention and that "formal guidelines, goals, reports, and follow-up procedures should be established so that management could maintain vigilance over [a continuing conversion] program and measure its achievements."[2] Nearly 50 years later, studies of military-to-civilian conversions offer strikingly similar assessments. Emerging best practices are described in greater detail below.

Use a Comprehensive Approach to Estimating Relative Personnel Costs

There is broad agreement across nearly all the studies reviewed that—in the case of non–military-essential yet inherently governmental activities, and under specified conditions—converting additional military positions to civilian positions could be beneficial and achieve substantial savings. Determining the relative cost of military and civilian manpower is not always straightforward, however. One approach researchers have taken is to develop comprehensive estimates of the total costs of an employee

---

[1] GAO, *Follow-Up Review on Use by the Coast Guard of Military Personnel in Civilian-Type Positions*, Washington, D.C., B-114851, 1969; GAO, *Extensive Use of Military Personnel in Civilian-Type Positions*, Washington, D.C., B-146890, 1972; GAO, *Using Civilian Personnel for Military Administrative and Support Positions—Can More Be Done?* Washington, D.C., B-146890, 1978; GAO, *Civilianizing Certain Air Force Positions Could Result in Economies and Better Use of Military Personnel*, Washington, D.C., B-207885, 1982; Palmer and Osbaldeston, 1988; and Gates and Robbert, 1998.

[2] GAO, 1969.

to the taxpayer.[3] Another approach is to compare only the elements of cost that differ between civilian and military personnel.[4]

Cost savings may not always be apparent to installation commanders or to DoD. CBO shows, for example, that while a DoD civilian occupying a commercial position costs the federal government about 30 percent less, on average, than a military service member in a similar position, the civilian may, in fact, cost DoD slightly more than the service member. As discussed in Chapter Four, active-duty service members often cost less to DoD than to the federal government as a whole because a significant portion of their costs is borne by other federal agencies, such as the Department of Veterans Affairs, the Department of the Treasury, the Office of Personnel Management, and the Department of Education.[5]

Estimates of relative personnel costs should therefore consider not only the costs borne by DoD but also the costs (and revenues) borne by other federal agencies. The estimates should reflect both direct and indirect costs, including the costs of recruitment, training, relocation, regular salaries or wages, additional pay (overtime, holiday pay, or duty-related special and incentive pays), and benefits (e.g., health care, life insurance, and retirement), as well as support costs and inventory flow costs (e.g., costs generated upon initial hire or separation). Cost comparisons should also reflect whether the income earned is fully taxable.

Differences in training requirements and differences in career length can often have a large influence on cost calculations. For example, whereas civilian linguists are often hired with native language proficiency and can therefore provide valuable services immediately, military linguists must be trained for at least two years, during which they represent more of a cost than a benefit.[6]

Analysts should also consider a sufficiently long time horizon to incorporate the career patterns and training requirements of different personnel types. Although many analyses account for the fact that military personnel tend to have shorter careers, few studies recognize that military personnel often go on to serve in civilian positions within the government, so there is a net contribution of the flow of military to civilian employment. For example, RAND studies have found that more than one-third of acquisition workforce civilian employees have prior military expe-

---

[3] See, for example, Asch and Winkler, 2013; and Kirsten M. Keller, Nelson Lim, Lisa M. Harrington, Kevin O'Neill, and Abigail Haddad, *The Mix of Military and Civilian Faculty at the United States Air Force Academy: Finding a Sustainable Balance for Enduring Success*, Santa Monica, Calif.: RAND Corporation, MG-1237-AF, 2013.

[4] See, for example, Gates and Robbert, 1998.

[5] CBO, 2015.

[6] Asch and Winkler, 2013.

rience.[7] Current DoD guidance does not indicate that this contribution should be incorporated. It therefore leads analysts to overstate the relative cost-effectiveness of civilians and understate the relative cost-effectiveness of military personnel.[8]

In addition, cost comparison studies should seek to understand the underlying factors that drive differences in labor costs and productivity—which is "not just the amount of work performed but also quality, timeliness, and responsiveness, which are determined by knowledge, skills, and abilities; availability and flexibility; incentives; and other factors."[9] Productivity increases with work effort in response to performance incentives, as well as technology, the operational environment, and the type and extent of complementary skills.[10] So, ideally, cost comparisons should also incorporate projected effects of recent policy changes, as well as technological or operational developments.

Finally, cost comparisons are dependent on military and civil service grade distributions and substitution ratios between military and civil service personnel. These may differ across position types and installations, and in practice, they may deviate from what is predicted at the start of a military-to-civilian conversion program. CBO presented the option of replacing three military positions with two civilian positions. Implementing this substitution ratio is more feasible in cases in which a large number of conversions are occurring at a single installation within a single occupation at roughly the same time. When only one or two conversions occur at a given installation within a particular occupation, substitutions tend to occur one for one (hiring 67 percent of a civilian is simply not practical). Errors in estimating the substitution ratio can sometimes lead to overestimates of the cost savings from conversions.

On the other hand, the case of DoD's conversions of military health care positions between 2005 and 2010 shows that substitution ratios may sometimes be lower than predicted, which can lead to underestimates of the cost savings. When DoD undertook the conversions of military health care positions, DoD officials assumed that the substitution ratio between military and civilian medical and dental personnel would need to be one for one. However, a Navy efficiency review ultimately determined that

---

[7] Susan M. Gates, Edward G. Keating, Adria D. Jewell, Lindsay Daugherty, Bryan Tysinger, Albert A. Robbert, and Ralph Masi, *The Defense Acquisition Workforce: An Analysis of Personnel Trends Relevant to Policy, 1993-2006*, Santa Monica, Calif.: RAND Corporation, TR-572-OSD, 2008.

[8] Asch and Winkler, 2013.

[9] Asch and Winkler, 2013.

[10] See, for example, Ronald D. Fricker, *The Effects of Perstempo on Officer Retention in the U.S. Military*, Santa Monica, Calif.: RAND Corporation, MR-1556-OSD, 2002; James Hosek and Mark E. Totten, *Serving Away from Home: How Deployments Influence Reenlistment*, Santa Monica, Calif.: RAND Corporation, MR-1594-OSD, 2002; and James Hosek and Francisco Martorell, *How Have Deployments During the War on Terrorism Affected Reenlistment?* Santa Monica, Calif.: RAND Corporation, MG-873-OSD, 2009.

the Navy did not need to hire one civilian to fill each converted position and that far fewer civilians than expected were required to provide the same capability.[11]

The data needed to answer pertinent staffing questions—such as which civilian grades are substituted for which military grades and how many civilian personnel must be substituted for one military personnel member—are often not available. Cost comparison studies should therefore rely on the literature and on historical data on past conversions to infer reasonable lower and upper bounds on cost predictions. The data described in Chapter Three of this report and the list of references provided in the bibliography can help to inform future studies.

Several DoD documents and scholarly studies present cost comparisons of military versus civilian employees in particular career fields using full cost methodologies. DoDI 7041.04 includes a sample cost comparison for a Department of the Army operations research analyst position in the Washington, D.C., metropolitan area, working at a government site. The example shows that the full cost to the government of a GS-14 civilian would be about 25 percent lower than that of an O-5 Army officer. A recent RAND study found that civilians are generally a more cost-effective source of language capability.[12] Another RAND study found that the least costly military faculty member at the U.S. Air Force Academy is more expensive than a civilian instructor.[13] A recent IDA study conducted cost calculations for Army medical enlisted soldiers, Navy physicians, and Air Force nurses and estimated that the full cost to the taxpayer of civilian medical personnel is about 25 percent to 40 percent less than that of equivalent military personnel.[14]

A number of studies have employed full cost methodologies to estimate the total savings that would result from a wave of military-to-civilian conversions. In a recent study, CBO found that if every service were to adopt the approach of the service with the smallest percentage of military personnel in each commercial occupation, about 80,000 active-duty positions would be available for conversion. Converting these positions could eventually save the federal government as a whole \$3.1 billion to \$5.7 billion per year.[15] IDA found that civilianizing Air Force and Navy military personnel until they reached the Army's overall ratio of civilian to military personnel would save the federal government about \$500 million per year in direct costs initially, and double that in the long run due to reductions in training costs, special pays, and overhead

---

[11] GAO, *Military Personnel: Guidance Needed for Any Future Conversions of Military Medical Positions to Civilian Positions*, Washington, D.C., GAO-08-370R, 2008.

[12] Asch and Winkler, 2013.

[13] Keller et al., 2013.

[14] Whitley et al., 2014.

[15] CBO, 2015. The lower estimate reflects a substitution ratio of one civilian for each service member, while the upper estimate reflects a ratio of two civilians for three service members.

requirements.[16] The earliest study we reviewed, a 1969 GAO report, identified 361 military Coast Guard billets as appropriate for conversion and found that the resulting savings would amount to about $550,000 annually.[17] While the full cost methodologies used and the amounts of money involved have changed over time, the key finding has remained consistent: Conversions can achieve considerable savings for the federal government as a whole.

Using comprehensive cost estimates can help DoD identify which positions are most appropriate for conversion and maximize savings. For example, a 2007 RAND study presents detailed estimates of the entire life-cycle stream of compensation and benefits and concludes that in order to maximize savings, conversion efforts should focus on positions in grades O-3 to O-5 for officers and grades E-5 through E-7 for enlisted personnel.[18]

While using full cost estimates may be a best practice, it is not always followed. During the conversion of military health care positions between 2005 and 2009, for example, GAO found that only the Navy was using a full cost methodology and including indirect costs in the documents it was submitting to Congress. The Air Force and Army were instead relying on composite military rates that did not account for such factors as training and recruitment.[19] As Whitley et al. show, the composite rate substantially understates the full cost of military personnel.[20]

Even when studies use full cost methodologies, however, there will be some uncertainty around the cost estimates caused by variation across organizations, locations, years, and individuals. Studies will inevitably have to rely on assumptions. Cost estimates may also be contingent on particular government policies or procedures. Wherever possible, analysts should clearly acknowledge the assumptions underlying their estimates and adjust them as policies or conditions change. For example, service personnel funding is based on aggregate strength estimates and programmed grade distributions, which do not change in response to changes in authorized grades. Thus, a reduction or conversion of an O-1 authorization has the same impact on funding as reduction or conversion of an O-6 authorization. As a result, Gates and Robbert found that there were "break-even" civil service grades, below which military-to-civilian conversions were cost-effective and above which they were not, and recommended that conversions be limited to positions that could be filled with lower-grade civil service

16 Horowitz, 2014.

17 GAO, 1969.

18 Carl J. Dahlman, *The Cost of a Military Person-Year: A Method for Computing Savings from Force Reductions*, Santa Monica, Calif.: MG-598-OSD, 2007.

19 GAO, 2008.

20 Whitley et al., 2014.

workers.[21] Changes in personnel funding procedures could lead to a different assessment, however.

DoDI 7041.04 on manpower costing and OSD CAPE's Full Cost of Manpower costing tool provide a strong foundation for the development of comprehensive cost comparison studies. However, analysts should modify these tools where necessary to account for the unique characteristics and requirements of different career fields. They should take a whole-of-government perspective and consider a sufficiently long time horizon. Where necessary, they should make appropriate assumptions based on the best available historical data and literature on past conversions.

Link Robust Personnel Data Collection Mechanisms to Budget and Workforce Planning Processes

The identification and execution of appropriate military-to-civilian conversions—as with workforce planning more generally—require an extensive array of data, as well as the capability to analyze the data and use the analysis to inform decisions.[22] The first challenge is collecting and maintaining appropriate data, which requires time and resources. It also requires creating incentives for managers to report information regularly and completely and investing in information technology systems and databases that are well maintained and frequently updated. The second challenge is developing the capacity to analyze the data in a timely and appropriate manner so that the analysis can inform budget and workforce planning processes.

As Nataraj et al. note, DoD workforce managers would ideally have access to a comprehensive centralized source of manpower data that identifies the occupation or function associated with each individual and position.[23] While the Defense Civilian Personnel Data System, the Civilian Personnel Master Files, the Active Duty Military Personnel Master File, the Work Experience File, and other databases maintained by DMDC and other DoD entities are rich sources of centralized data, numerous studies have identified important gaps.

For example, there is little systematic data collection on personnel skills and competencies or on competency requirements and customer demand.[24] Options for linking

---

[21] Gates and Robbert, 1998.

[22] Robert M. Emmerichs, Cheryl Y. Marcum, and Albert A. Robbert, *An Executive Perspective on Workforce Planning*, Santa Monica, Calif.: RAND Corporation, MR-1684/2-OSD, 2004.

[23] Shanthi Nataraj, Christopher Guo, Philip Hall-Partyka, Susan M. Gates, and Douglas Yeung, *Options for Department of Defense Total Workforce Supply and Demand Analysis: Potential Approaches and Available Data Sources*, Santa Monica, Calif.: RAND Corporation, RR-543-OSD, 2014.

[24] Nataraj et al., 2014; Susan M. Gates, Christine Eibner, and Edward G. Keating, *Civilian Workforce Planning in the Department of Defense: Different Levels, Different Roles*, Santa Monica, Calif.: RAND Corporation, MG-449-OSD, 2006.

manpower and workforce data to analyze functional communities or occupations are limited.[25] Training cost data are particularly difficult to find,[26] and there is an urgent need for the development of annual training cost estimates by specialty.[27] There is little reliable data on the usage rates and costs of particular incentive programs and benefits.[28] And there is a dearth of data on the number of contractors, their costs, and the functions actually performed.[29] An added challenge is that some categorizations of DoD personnel in existing databases turn out to be administrative (e.g., acquisition or cyber), not substantive, so it can be difficult to identify who makes up the workforce, let alone to analyze or reshape it.[30]

The various elements of personnel compensation that make up total personnel costs are not easily identified in budget displays, even at the aggregate level. Instead, they have to be cobbled together from various parts of the federal budget. Several researchers have recommended that DoD move more of the cost of military personnel into the military personnel appropriation so that researchers can more easily see it.[31] Ideally, cost comparison studies should use occupation- and pay grade–specific data since retention rates, deployment rates, moving costs, training costs, and other important characteristics can vary significantly across the force. Even when researchers are able to calculate the average cost of a military or civilian person-year, this information is often of little use in practice for informing military-to-civilian conversions, because particular instances of proposed conversions are likely to deviate substantially from the average.

Finally, budget estimates may not be the ideal data source for evaluating the effects of past conversions and informing assessments of future conversions. Because budget projections can sometimes diverge quite sharply from actual expenditures, execution data, which are more difficult to find, may be more informative about the actual costs of conversions.

Several past studies contain recommendations for ways in which OSD can improve data collection and analytical processes.[32] The studies also acknowledge the

---

[25] Nataraj et al., 2014.

[26] Asch and Winkler, 2013.

[27] Horowitz, 2014.

[28] Dahlman, 2007.

[29] Riposo et al., 2011.

[30] Gates et al., 2008.

[31] GAO, *Military Personnel: DoD Needs to Improve the Transparency and Reassess the Reasonableness, Appropriateness, Affordability, and Sustainability of Its Military Compensation System*, Washington, D.C., GAO-05-798, 2005; Dahlman, 2007; and Horowitz, 2014.

[32] GAO, 2008; GAO, *Human Capital: Further Actions Needed to Enhance DOD's Civilian Strategic Workforce Plan*, Washington, D.C., GAO-10-814R, 2010; GAO, *DOD Civilian Personnel: Competency Gap Analyses and Other Actions Needed to Enhance DOD's Strategic Workforce Plans*, Washington, D.C., GAO-11-827T, 2011;

substantial costs and investments that will be required to make these improvements and present frameworks for assessing whether the potential benefits warrant the costs. The most thorough discussion of options for improving data systems and the trade-offs inherent in each can be found in a report by Nataraj et al., which presents short-term, medium-term, and long-term options for addressing data limitations and discusses the costs and benefits of each.[33] The study includes potential survey questions and describes numerous approaches and specific tools that are available to help workforce planners become more effective. In their 2013 report on language capability in the Intelligence Community, Asch and Winkler also provide decisionmakers with descriptions of the data they need to determine the optimal mix of military and civilian personnel.[34] They list the elements required to estimate cost comparison models and provide the websites that yield the data for estimating these elements. The key difference between the studies is that Nataraj et al. focus more heavily on describing the data required for demand, supply, and competency gap analysis, whereas Asch and Winkler focus more specifically on the data required for cost analyses and comparisons across personnel categories.

GAO has outlined a number of improvements that DoD could make to the way it collects and tracks data on personnel skills and competencies and conducts gap analysis for mission-critical occupations. GAO also recommends refinements to the policies and procedures DoD uses for determining optimal workforce mix and developing strategic workforce plans.[35]

Critical Skill and Competency Gap Assessments Offer Useful Insights for Workforce Mix Decisions

As the services improve data collection on personnel demand, supply, competencies, and costs, they will become better able to inform OSD's policies and budget decisions and to respond to various constraints. Likewise, if DoD improves its data collection processes, it may be more successful in influencing congressional personnel policies.

When Congress or OSD impose constraints on civilian hiring or retention, the services and various DoD components could use critical skill and competency gap

---

GAO, *DOD Needs Complete Assessments to Improve Future Civilian Strategic Workforce Plans*, Washington, D.C., GAO-12-1014, 2012; GAO, *Additional Steps Needed to Help Determine the Right Size and Composition of DOD's Total Workforce*, Washington, D.C., GAO-13-470, 2013a; GAO, 2013b; Gates, Eibner, and Keating, 2006; and Albert A. Robbert, Lisa M. Harrington, Tara L. Terry, and H. G. Massey, *Air Force Manpower Requirements and Component Mix: A Focus on Agile Combat Support*, Santa Monica, Calif.: RAND Corporation, RR-617-AF, 2014.

33 Nataraj et al., 2014.

34 Asch and Winkler, 2013.

35 GAO, 2012; GAO, 2013a; GAO, 2013b; and U.S. Government Accountability Office, *DOD Should Fully Develop Its Civilian Strategic Workforce Plan to Aid Decision Makers*, Washington, D.C., GAO-14-565, 2014b.

assessments to prioritize among positions and develop strategies to mitigate skill shortages that jeopardize mission accomplishment.[36] Such assessments should also inform the process that DoD components use to request exceptions to constraints, such as civilian personnel caps. OSD has granted exceptions under certain circumstances during past caps. For example, when the number of civilian FTE personnel was capped at FY 2010 levels for FY 2011–2013, DoD granted exceptions for the acquisition workforce because shortages of trained acquisition personnel were undermining the department's ability to supervise contracts.[37] The services' acquisition workforces could demonstrate critical gaps partly because they collect more detailed personnel data than other functional communities do.

In 2010, DoD identified the need to increase its acquisition workforce by 20,000 personnel by FY 2015 but failed to meet many of the requirements outlined in the FY 2010 NDAA.[38] DoD neither conducted an assessment of the skills and competencies of its existing acquisition workforce; nor assessed the appropriate mix of military service members, government civilian personnel, and contracts for services in its total acquisition workforce; nor estimated the funding needed to increase the workforce. On the basis of correspondence with members of Congress, GAO determined that DoD was likely to be far more successful in achieving desired changes to statutory personnel authorizations and budgets if it were to collect appropriate data and conduct pertinent assessments of critical capability gaps.[39] As a general rule, DoD services and agencies may have greater success in influencing OSD policies and budget requests and encouraging Congress to relax hiring constraints if they can demonstrate clearly what their organizations' competency requirements are and where the key gaps exist.

Centralized Guidance Can Inform Workforce Assessments and Planning

Congress has been calling for DoD to develop a more fully integrated workforce analysis and planning system since the 1970s, if not before.[40] Although DoD has developed broad guidance, GAO and RAND reports have repeatedly found that the department does not have adequate policies and procedures in place to assess the appropriate work-

---

36 GAO, 2011; GAO, 2012; and GAO, 2013b.

37 GAO, 2013b.

38 GAO, 2011.

39 GAO, 2011.

40 M. Letsky, R. J. Niehaus, and J. W. Shaddy, *Integrated Military-Civilian Workforce Analysis and Planning*, Washington, D.C.: Office of Civilian Manpower Management, Department of the Navy, Research Report No. 28, 1978.

force mix or to guide DoD components in making appropriate workforce mix decisions and changes.

Although military and civilian personnel often work side by side, sometimes doing similar jobs, military and civilian workforce analysis and planning processes have traditionally been fragmented and poorly integrated. While there are several relevant DoD instructions and directives, there is still considerable confusion about how such guidance should be interpreted and implemented in practice.

In 2006, RAND explored how civilian workforce planning and requirements determination are accomplished at specific installations and at the service, agency, command, and department levels.[41] The study found that DoD lacks department-wide workforce planning and requirements determination processes for the civilian workforce—let alone an integrated process for determining the best mix of military service members, government civilian personnel, and contracts for services. It recommended a logical four-step process for conducting workforce analyses but cautioned that, in practice, each of these steps is complicated and requires new data collection efforts and changes to workforce management practices:

- Step 1: Forecast demand. Estimate staffing levels and competencies required in the future workforce—and develop *workforce requirements* (i.e., the number of positions and characteristics of workers required).
- Step 2: Project supply. Project current staffing levels and competency profiles into the future based on current trends in hiring, attrition, and retention.
- Step 3: Identify gaps between supply and demand.
- Step 4: Develop strategies to address the key gaps.

Workforce planners are limited in their ability to follow such a process by insufficient data on competencies and skills and uncertainty regarding customer demand, among other challenges.[42]

For example, in their 2014 report, Robbert et al. found that some of the Air Force's manpower requirements determination practices were decades old, poorly validated, and inconsistent and contained inadequate linkages between the active and reserve components and between wartime and peacetime requirements.[43] The authors faulted insufficient oversight and guidance, as well as the devotion of insufficient resources to the development of manpower standards and other requirements processes. Because of these insufficiencies, functional managers at the service headquarters tasked with managing the workforce in a particular career field tend to assess demands independently

---

41 Gates, Eibner, and Keating, 2006.

42 Gates, Eibner, and Keating, 2006; Gates et al., 2008.

43 Robbert et al., 2014.

and subjectively without common planning assumptions, institutionalized processes for coordinating across organizations, or centralized leadership.

Several studies suggest improvements that could be made to workforce management practices to address these challenges. At the service level, Scott et al. outline a five-step strategic approach to human capital management that they argue would improve the Air Force's management of its cyber force,[44] and Reed proposes a model for analyzing and managing the Army's contracting workforce.[45] At the department level, GAO has made numerous recommendations regarding DoD's Strategic Workforce Plan and has focused on the need for improving DoD's compliance with statutory reporting requirements, clarifying DoD guidance to the services, and enhancing performance measures.[46]

Riposo et al. outline a methodology for implementing current DoD guidance on in-sourcing and provide user-friendly resources, such as questionnaires about the civilian-contractor mix of the workforce.[47] Such resources could be adapted and used to collect data on the military-civilian workforce mix and to make assessments regarding which positions are appropriate for civilianization. Another RAND report by Asch and Winkler provides broad guidance for decisionmakers on what factors to consider as they assess the optimum workforce mix.[48] Further work is required to translate sound workforce planning processes and principles into clear guidelines that are tailored to each service and career field.

Devote Increased Attention to the Education, Training, Professional Development, and Compensation of Civilian Personnel

A DoD program to conduct additional military-to-civilian conversions would likely benefit from efforts to improve the overall health of the civilian workforce. DoD will need to attract new civilian hires into converted positions and retain them long enough to reap the cost benefits. There is a large literature dealing with steps that DoD can take to improve recruitment, retention, and expertise in the civilian workforce.

In particular, DoD should support the development of more flexible compensation schemes for the civilian workforce. A limited number of such projects were initially authorized under the 1978 Civil Service Reform Act, which allowed federal agencies

---

44 Lynn M. Scott, Raymond E. Conley, Richard Mesic, Edward O'Connell, and Darren D. Medlin, *Human Capital Management for the USAF Cyber Force*, Santa Monica, Calif.: RAND Corporation, DB-579-AF, 2010.

45 Timothy Reed, *Army Contracting Command Workforce Model Analysis*, Monterey, Calif.: Acquisition Program, Graduate School of Business and Public Policy, Naval Postgraduate School, NPS-CM-10-179, 2010.

46 GAO, 2014b.

47 Riposo et al., 2011.

48 Asch and Winkler, 2013.

to set up alternatives to the General Schedule (GS) pay system so that they could test and evaluate alternative approaches to managing their human capital.[49] There is some evidence that personnel who enter under a demonstration pay plan, such as the Acquisition Workforce Personnel Demonstration Project (AcqDemo), are retained longer than those in the GS plan.[50] DoD could consider expanding and refining demonstration pay plans with more flexible compensation schemes to support recruitment and retention in the civilian workforce.

Increasing investment in in-house training for civilians,[51] encouraging civilians to pursue higher education while in DoD service,[52] and increasing attention to the development of attractive advancement opportunities[53] are other steps that could improve the health of the civilian workforce.

DoD may also need to address declining morale in the civilian workforce, since low morale could harm DoD's ability to attract new civilian hires into converted positions. Observers note that civilian morale has been declining since 2010,[54] largely because of pay freezes, furloughs, civilian hiring freezes, limits on overtime, and increases in the retirement contribution rate.[55] To the extent that poor morale reduces retention, it could erode key advantages that the civilian workforce has over the mili-

---

[49] GAO, *Implementing Pay for Performance at Selected Personnel Demonstration Projects*, Washington, D.C., GAO-04-83, 2004.

[50] Christopher Guo, Philip Hall-Partyka, and Susan M. Gates, *Retention and Promotion of High-Quality Civil Service Workers in the Department of Defense Acquisition Workforce*, Santa Monica, Calif.: RAND Corporation, RR-748-OSD, 2014; and Laura Werber, Lindsay Daugherty, Edward G. Keating, and Matthew Hoover, *An Assessment of the Civilian Acquisition Workforce Personnel Demonstration Project*, Santa Monica, Calif.: RAND Corporation, TR-1286-OSD, 2012.

[51] George Vernez and H. G. Massey, *The Acquisition Cost-Estimating Workforce: Census and Characteristics*, Santa Monica, Calif.: RAND Corporation, TR-708-AF, 2009.

[52] Guo, Hall-Partyka, and Gates, 2014.

[53] Vernez and Massey, 2009.

[54] The Office of Personnel Management's annual Federal Employee Viewpoint Survey shows a decline among DoD respondents in job satisfaction (71 percent in 2010 versus 65 percent in 2015), satisfaction with pay (65 percent in 2010 versus 57 percent in 2015), and satisfaction with the organization (63 percent in 2010 versus 56 percent in 2015). However, satisfaction levels have risen slightly since their 2013–2014 lows. See U.S. Office of Personnel Management, *2013 Federal Employee Viewpoint Survey Results: Employees Influencing Change*, Department of Defense Agency Management Report, Washington, D.C., 2013; and U.S. Office of Personnel Management, *2015 Federal Employee Viewpoint Survey Results: Employees Influencing Change*, Department of Defense Agency Management Report, Washington, D.C., 2015.

[55] Beth J. Asch, Michael G. Mattock, and James Hosek, *The Federal Civil Service Workforce: Assessing the Effects on Retention of Pay Freezes, Unpaid Furloughs, and Other Federal-Employee Compensation Changes in the Department of Defense*, Santa Monica, Calif.: RAND Corporation, RR-514-OSD, 2014a; GAO, *Comprehensive and Updated Cost Savings Would Better Inform DOD Decision Makers If Future Civilian Furloughs Occur*, Washington, D.C., GAO-14-529, 2014a; and GAO, 2014b.

tary workforce (e.g., less churn and lower training costs) and thereby undermine the very rationale for conversions.[56]

Ensure That Military-to-Civilian Conversions Are Supported by DoD Budget Requests and Justifications

Congressionally mandated reductions in the number of civilian employees authorized to DoD—and, in the case of health care workers, an explicit statutory prohibition on military-to-civilian conversions—have on several occasions over the past 50 years interrupted, delayed, or discouraged the implementation of conversions. The Revenue and Expenditure Control Act of 1968 had lasting effects,[57] as did the civilian drawdown of the 1990s.[58] More recently, the FY 2013 NDAA, which required that DoD's efficiencies plan achieve savings in total funding of the civilian and service contractor workforces that were not less than certain savings achieved from reductions in military end strength, has been perceived as somewhat inconsistent with continued military-to-civilian conversions.[59]

In many cases, however, DoD might have been able to secure higher numbers of civilian personnel authorizations had it been prepared to reduce military authorizations and provide OMB and Congress with clear justification for conversions of specific positions. Furthermore, many of the restrictions on civilian hiring within DoD have been self-imposed. For example, it was the Secretary of Defense who capped the number of civilian FTEs at the FY 2010 level for FYs 2012–2013 as part of an efficiency initiative.[60]

If DoD determines that further military-to-civilian conversions are appropriate, and if it seeks the support of OMB and Congress in authorizing those conversions, it is essential that DoD provide clear and comprehensive justifications for each particular set of conversions. Moreover, DoD should explicitly request adjustments to the relevant authorizations and appropriations necessary to accommodate the desired conversions.

---

[56] Results from RAND simulation models show that the 2011–2013 pay freeze may reduce retention of civilian employees by about 7.3 percent in the long run and that increases in the retirement contribution rate for civilian employees hired after 2012 may reduce retention by up to 8.6 percent in the long run. See Beth J. Asch, Michael G. Mattock, and James Hosek, *How Do Federal Civilian Pay Freezes and Retirement Plan Changes Affect Employee Retention in the Department of Defense?* Santa Monica, Calif.: RAND Corporation, RR-678-OSD, 2014b; and Asch, Mattock, and Hosek, 2014a.

[57] GAO, 1978.

[58] GAO, *DoD Force Mix Issues: Converting Some Support Officer Positions to Civilian Status Could Save Money*, Washington, D.C., NSIAD-97-15, 1996.

[59] GAO, 2013a.

[60] GAO, 2013b.

After identifying positions appropriate for conversion and conducting comprehensive cost-benefit analyses, DoD could provide OMB with realistic estimates of the numbers of military positions that could be converted to civilian positions, along with justifications for the number of civilian positions that would need to be retained or added to accomplish the mission successfully. Finally, DoD could collect the relevant data that would allow Congress to exercise oversight, evaluate the effects of executed conversions, and change course where necessary.

APPENDIX B

Methodology for Expert Elicitation

The Director, Total Force Planning and Requirements, OUSD(P&R), asked RAND to identify the primary impediments to converting military positions to functions that can be performed by government civilians. As part of this effort, RAND researchers conducted a series of discussions (either in person or via telephone) with subject matter experts inside and outside DoD on a nonattribution basis. The initial set of experts was identified by reaching out to established contacts within RAND, OSD, and the services and requesting referrals to manpower experts with knowledge of the military-to-civilian conversion process. Additional experts were identified by soliciting referrals at the conclusion of each discussion.

We employed a qualitatively based, expert elicitation research method to glean information from each respondent. We used a semi-structured approach and conducted a total of 21 discussions, each of which lasted approximately one hour. We conducted 11 discussions with U.S. Navy–related personnel, four with experts in OSD, three with U.S. Army–related personnel, two with U.S. Air Force–related personnel, and one with a U.S. Marine Corps–related expert.

The subject matter experts were asked the following questions:

- What are your professional responsibilities? Which of those responsibilities involve military-to-civilian conversions? Have you had previous positions that have also related to military-to-civilian conversions?
- Describe your specific experiences with military-to-civilian conversions.
- Which positions are best suited to conversions? What are the benefits of these conversions? What are the drawbacks?
- Which positions are least suited to conversions? Why?
- What is the process by which conversions are implemented?
  - What is the process by which positions are identified for conversion?
  - What is the process by which military positions are eliminated?
  - What is the process by which a civilian or contractor is brought in to perform the functions that were previously associated with the now defunct military position?

  - Is a new civilian position created, or are those functions assigned to government civilians occupying existing positions?
  - Is a new contractor hired, or are the functions assigned to an existing contractor?
- Which policies or statutes do you look toward for guidance on military-to-civilian conversions?
- In your experience, which policies, statutes, or business practices bear most heavily on military-to-civilian conversions?
- Do you have any experiences with desired conversions that were thwarted? If so, please describe them. What were the primary impediments?
- RAND has obtained the following figures from an OSD report [Table B.1]:

Table B.1
Military-to-Civilian Conversions (Number of Military Personnel Converted)

Component	FY 2008	FY 2009	FY 2010	Change FY 2009–2010
Army	14,523	14,662	14,690	28
Navy	15,682	17,258	19,110	1,852
Marine Corps	3,811	4,111	4,436	325
Air Force	8,240	8,875	10,070	1,195
Total	42,256	44,906	48,306	3,400

- The source of these figures is the OSD Operation and Maintenance Overview, Fiscal Year 2010 Budget Estimates, published in May 2009 and revised in June 2009. Do you know how the figures were obtained or calculated? If not, are you able to refer us to someone who might know how the figures were obtained or calculated?
- Are there references/sources about military-to-civilian conversions that you recommend?
- Are there other subject matter experts, either within your organization or outside of it, whom you recommend we talk to?
- Are there other issues related to military-to-civilian conversions that we haven't mentioned that are also important?

In most cases, follow-up questions were asked to solicit additional details regarding the expert's initial response. The set of discussion questions listed above was reviewed by RAND's Human Subjects Protection Committee and by the DoD second-level review process.

Bibliography

Works Cited

Asch, Beth J., Michael G. Mattock, and James Hosek, *The Federal Civil Service Workforce: Assessing the Effects on Retention of Pay Freezes, Unpaid Furloughs, and Other Federal-Employee Compensation Changes in the Department of Defense*, Santa Monica, Calif.: RAND Corporation, RR-514-OSD, 2014a. As of August 18, 2015:
http://www.rand.org/pubs/research_reports/RR514

———, *How Do Federal Civilian Pay Freezes and Retirement Plan Changes Affect Employee Retention in the Department of Defense?* Santa Monica, Calif.: RAND Corporation, RR-678-OSD, 2014b. As of August 18, 2015:
http://www.rand.org/pubs/research_reports/RR678

Asch, Beth J., and John D. Winkler, *Ensuring Language Capability in the Intelligence Community: What Factors Affect the Best Mix of Military, Civilians, and Contractors?* Santa Monica, Calif.: RAND Corporation, TR-1284-ODNI, 2013. As of May 1, 2016:
http://www.rand.org/pubs/technical_reports/TR1284.html

CBO—*see* Congressional Budget Office.

Commandant of the Marine Corps, Marine Corps Order 5311.1D, *Total Force Structure Process (TFSP)*, 2009.

———, Marine Corps Order 12250.2, *Civilian Command-Level Strategic Workforce Planning Procedures*, 2014.

Congressional Budget Office, *Options for Reducing the Deficit: 2014 to 2023*, Washington, D.C., Pub. No. 4664, November 2013. As of July 28, 2015:
http://www.cbo.gov/sites/default/files/cbofiles/attachments/44715-OptionsForReducingDeficit-3.pdf

———, *Replacing Military Personnel in Support Positions with Civilian Employees*, Washington, D.C., Pub. No. 51012, December 2015. As of December 6, 2015:
https://www.cbo.gov/publication/51012.

Dahlman, Carl J., *The Cost of a Military Person-Year: A Method for Computing Savings from Force Reductions*, Santa Monica, Calif.: RAND Corporation, MG-598-OSD, 2007. As of May 1, 2016:
http://www.rand.org/pubs/monographs/MG598.html

Department of the Army, Army Regulation 570-4, *Manpower Management*, 2006.

DoD—*see* U.S. Department of Defense.

DoDD—*see* U.S. Department of Defense Directive.

DoDI—*see* U.S. Department of Defense Instruction.

Dunigan, Molly, Todd Nichols, Michael Schwille, Susanne Sondergaard, and Susan S. Everingham, *Expeditionary Civilians: Creating a Viable Practice of Civilian Deployment Within the Department of Defense*, Santa Monica, Calif.: RAND Corporation, RR-975-OSD, 2016. As of June 15, 2016: http://www.rand.org/pubs/research_reports/RR975.html

Emmerichs, Robert M., Cheryl Y. Marcum, and Albert A. Robbert, *An Executive Perspective on Workforce Planning*, Santa Monica, Calif.: RAND Corporation, MR-1684/2-OSD, 2004. As of May 1, 2016: http://www.rand.org/pubs/monograph_reports/MR1684z2.html

Fricker, Ronald D., *The Effects of Perstempo on Officer Retention in the U.S. Military*, Santa Monica, Calif.: RAND Corporation, MR-1556-OSD, 2002. As of May 1, 2016: http://www.rand.org/pubs/monograph_reports/MR1556.html

GAO—*see* U.S. Government Accountability Office or U.S. General Accounting Office.

Gates, Susan M., Christine Eibner, and Edward G. Keating, *Civilian Workforce Planning in the Department of Defense: Different Levels, Different Roles*, Santa Monica, Calif.: RAND Corporation, MG-449-OSD, 2006. As of May 1, 2016: http://www.rand.org/pubs/monographs/MG449.html

Gates, Susan M., Edward G. Keating, Adria D. Jewell, Lindsay Daugherty, Bryan Tysinger, Albert A. Robbert, and Ralph Masi, *The Defense Acquisition Workforce: An Analysis of Personnel Trends Relevant to Policy, 1993–2006*, Santa Monica, Calif.: RAND Corporation, TR-572-OSD, 2008. As of May 1, 2016: http://www.rand.org/pubs/technical_reports/TR572.html

Gates, Susan M., and Albert A. Robbert, *Comparing the Costs of DoD Military and Civil Service Personnel*, Santa Monica, Calif.: RAND Corporation, MR-980-OSD, 1998. As of May 1, 2016: http://www.rand.org/pubs/monograph_reports/MR980.html

Guo, Christopher, Philip Hall-Partyka, and Susan M. Gates, *Retention and Promotion of High-Quality Civil Service Workers in the Department of Defense Acquisition Workforce*, Santa Monica, Calif.: RAND Corporation, RR-748-OSD, 2014. As of May 1, 2016: http://www.rand.org/pubs/research_reports/RR748.html

Horowitz, Stanley A., *Potential Savings from Substituting Civilians for Military Personnel (A Presentation)*, Alexandria, Va.: Institute for Defense Analyses, IDA Document NS D-5193, 2014.

Hosek, James, and Francisco Martorell, *How Have Deployments During the War on Terrorism Affected Reenlistment?* Santa Monica, Calif.: RAND Corporation, MG-873-OSD, 2009. As of May 1, 2016: http://www.rand.org/pubs/monographs/MG873.html

Hosek, James, and Mark E. Totten, *Serving Away from Home: How Deployments Influence Reenlistment*, Santa Monica, Calif.: RAND Corporation, MR-1594-OSD, 2002. As of May 1, 2016: http://www.rand.org/pubs/monograph_reports/MR1594.html

Katz, Eric, "Republican Lawmakers Want to Cut 115,000 Civilian Defense Jobs," *Government Executive*, March 17, 2014. As of April 16, 2015: http://www.govexec.com/defense/2014/03/republican-lawmakers-want-cut-115000-jobs-defense-department/80680/

Keller, Kirsten M., Nelson Lim, Lisa M. Harrington, Kevin O'Neill, and Abigail Haddad, *The Mix of Military and Civilian Faculty at the United States Air Force Academy: Finding a Sustainable Balance for Enduring Success*, Santa Monica, Calif.: RAND Corporation, MG-1237-AF, 2013. As of May 2, 2016: http://www.rand.org/pubs/monographs/MG1237.html

Letsky, M., R. J. Niehaus, and J. W. Shaddy, *Integrated Military-Civilian Workforce Analysis and Planning*, Washington, D.C.: Office of Civilian Manpower Management, Department of the Navy, Research Report No. 28, 1978.

Libicki, Martin C., David Senty, and Julia Pollak, *Hackers Wanted: An Examination of the Cybersecurity Labor Market*, Santa Monica, Calif.: RAND Corporation, RR-430, 2014. As of May 2, 2016:
http://www.rand.org/pubs/research_reports/RR430.html

Miller, Carl W., III, *The Programming and Budgeting Processes of the United States Marine Corps: An Investigation into Their Efficiency*, Monterey, Calif.: Naval Postgraduate School, thesis, 1999.

Nataraj, Shanthi, Christopher Guo, Philip Hall-Partyka, Susan M. Gates, and Douglas Yeung, *Options for Department of Defense Total Workforce Supply and Demand Analysis: Potential Approaches and Available Data Sources*, Santa Monica, Calif.: RAND Corporation, RR-543-OSD, 2014. As of May 2, 2016:
http://www.rand.org/pubs/research_reports/RR543.html

Office of the Chief of Naval Operations, OPNAV Instruction 1000.16L, *Navy Total Force Manpower Policies and Procedures*, 2015.

Office of Management and Budget, Circular A-76 (Revised), 2003.

———, Office of Federal Procurement Policy, *Policy Letter 11-01—Performance of Inherently Governmental and Other Critical Functions*, Federal Register, Vol. 76, No. 176, 2011, pp. 56227–56229.

Office of the Secretary of the Air Force, Air Force Policy Document 38-2, *Manpower*, March 2, 1995.

———, Air Force Manual 38-208, Vol. 1, *Air Force Management Engineering Program (MEP)—Processes*, 2007.

———, Air Force Instruction 38-201, *Management of Manpower Requirements and Authorizations*, 2014.

Office of the Secretary of Defense, *Operation and Maintenance Overview Fiscal Year (FY) 2010 Budget Estimates*, June 2009. As of June 15, 2016:
http://comptroller.defense.gov/Portals/45/Documents/defbudget/fy2010/fy2010_OM_Overview.pdf

OMB—*see* Office of Management and Budget.

OPNAV—*see* Office of the Chief of Naval Operations.

OSD—*see* Office of the Secretary of Defense.

Palmer, Adele R., James H. Bigelow, Joseph G. Bolten, Deena Dizengoff, Jennifer H. Kawata, H. G. Massey, Robert Petruschell, and Michael G. Shanley, *Assessing the Structure and Mix of Future Active and Reserve Forces: Cost Estimation Methodology*, Santa Monica, Calif.: RAND Corporation, MR-134-1-OSD, 1992. As of May 2, 2016:
http://www.rand.org/pubs/monograph_reports/MR134-1.html

Palmer, Adele R., and David J. Osbaldeston, *Incremental Costs of Military and Civilian Manpower in the Military Services*, Santa Monica, Calif.: RAND Corporation, N-2677-FMP, 1988. As of May 2, 2016:
http://www.rand.org/pubs/notes/N2677.html

Public Law 105-270, *Federal Activities Inventory Reform Act of 1998*, October 19, 1998.

Public Law 109-364, *National Defense Authorization Act for Fiscal Year 2007*, October 17, 2006.

Public Law 110-181, *National Defense Authorization Act for Fiscal Year 2008*, January 28, 2008.

Public Law 111-8, *Omnibus Appropriations Act, 2009*, March 11, 2009.

Public Law 111-84, *National Defense Authorization Act for Fiscal Year 2010*, October 28, 2009.

Public Law 112-239, *National Defense Authorization Act for Fiscal Year 2013*, January 2, 2013.

Public Law 114-133, *Consolidated Appropriations Act, 2016*, December 18, 2015.

Reed, Timothy, *Army Contracting Command Workforce Model Analysis*, Monterey, Calif.: Acquisition Program, Graduate School of Business and Public Policy, Naval Postgraduate School, NPS-CM-10-179, 2010.

Riposo, Jessie, Irv Blickstein, Stephanie Young, Geoffrey McGovern, and Brian McInnis, *A Methodology for Implementing the Department of Defense's Current In-Sourcing Policy*, Santa Monica, Calif.: RAND Corporation, TR-944-NAVY, 2011. As of May 2, 2016:
http://www.rand.org/pubs/technical_reports/TR944.html

Robbert, Albert A., Susan M. Gates, and Marc N. Elliott, *Outsourcing of DoD Commercial Activities: Impacts on Civil Service Employees*, Santa Monica, Calif.: RAND Corporation, MR-866-OSD, 1997. As of May 2, 2016:
http://www.rand.org/pubs/monograph_reports/MR866.html

Robbert, Albert A., Lisa M. Harrington, Tara L. Terry, and H. G. Massey, *Air Force Manpower Requirements and Component Mix: A Focus on Agile Combat Support*, Santa Monica, Calif.: RAND Corporation, RR-617-AF, 2014. As of May 2, 2016:
http://www.rand.org/pubs/research_reports/RR617.html

Rodney, David M., Michael D. Bowes, Christopher M. Duquette, and Sara M. Russell, with Kletus S. Lawler and Jessica S. Oi, *Impact of Manning and Infrastructure Initiatives on the Surface Navy*, Arlington, Va.: CNA, CRM D0021247.A2, 2009.

Scott, Lynn M., Raymond E. Conley, Richard Mesic, Edward O'Connell, and Darren D. Medlin, *Human Capital Management for the USAF Cyber Force*, Santa Monica, Calif.: RAND Corporation, DB-579-AF, 2010. As of August 17, 2015:
http://www.rand.org/pubs/documented_briefings/DB579

Secretary of Defense, *Department of Defense (DoD) Efficiency Initiatives*, memorandum, August 16, 2010a.

———, *Guidance on DoD Efficiency Initiatives with Immediate Application*, memorandum, August 20, 2010b.

Serbu, Jared, "Carter Opens Door to More DoD Civilian Job Cuts," Federal News Radio, March 5, 2015. As of April 16, 2015:
http://www.federalnewsradio.com/394/3812543/Carter-opens-door-to-more-DoD-civilian-job-cuts

United States Code, Title 5, Section 306, *Agency Strategic Plans*.

———, Title 10, Section 115(a), *Annual Defense Manpower Requirements Report*.

———, Title 10, Section 115(b), *Biennial Strategic Workforce Plan*.

———, Title 10, Section 129(a), *General Policy for Total Force Management*.

———, Title 10, Section 129(b), *Authority to Procure Personal Services*.

———, Title 10, Section 129(c), *Medical Personnel: Limitations on Reductions*.

———, Title 10, Section 143, *Office of the Secretary of Defense Personnel: Limitation*.

———, Title 10, Section 194, *Limitations on Personnel*.

———, Title 10, Section 1580, *Emergency Essential Employees: Designation*.

———, Title 10, Section 3014, *Office of the Secretary of the Army.*

———, Title 10, Section 5014, *Office of the Secretary of the Navy.*

———, Title 10, Section 8014, *Office of the Secretary of the Air Force.*

U.S.C.—*see* United States Code.

U.S. Congress, House of Representatives, Committee on Armed Services, *Civilian Workforce Requirements—Now and Across the Future Years Defense Program*, hearing before the Subcommittee on Readiness of the Committee on Armed Services, House of Representatives, One Hundred Twelfth Congress, second session, hearing held July 26, 2012, Washington, D.C.: U.S. Government Printing Office, 2013.

U.S. Department of Defense, Office of the Under Secretary of Defense, Personnel and Readiness, *Occupational Conversion Index: Enlisted/Officer/Civilian*, DoD 1312.1-1, March 2001. As of March 13, 2015:
http://www.dtic.mil/whs/directives/corres/pdf/131201i.pdf

———, Department of Defense Directive 1100.4, *Guidance for Manpower Programs*, 2005.

———, Department of Defense Instruction 1100.22, *Policy and Procedures for Determining Workforce Mix*, 2010.

———, Department of Defense Instruction 7041.04, *Estimating and Comparing the Full Costs of Civilian and Active Duty Military Manpower and Contract Support*, 2013. As of August 4, 2015:
http://dtic.mil/whs/directives/corres/pdf/704104p.pdf

U.S. General Accounting Office, *Follow-Up Review on Use by the Coast Guard of Military Personnel in Civilian-Type Positions*, Washington, D.C., B-114851, 1969.

——— *Extensive Use of Military Personnel in Civilian-Type Positions*, Washington, D.C., B-146890, 1972.

———, *Using Civilian Personnel for Military Administrative and Support Positions—Can More Be Done?* Washington, D.C., B-146890, 1978.

———, *Civilianizing Certain Air Force Positions Could Result in Economies and Better Use of Military Personnel*, Washington, D.C., B-207885, 1982.

———, *DoD Force Mix Issues: Converting Some Support Officer Positions to Civilian Status Could Save Money*, Washington, D.C., NSIAD-97-15, 1996.

———, *Implementing Pay for Performance at Selected Personnel Demonstration Projects*, Washington, D.C., GAO-04-83, 2004.

U.S. Government Accountability Office, *Military Personnel: DoD Needs to Improve the Transparency and Reassess the Reasonableness, Appropriateness, Affordability, and Sustainability of Its Military Compensation System*, Washington, D.C., GAO-05-798, 2005.

———, *Military Personnel: Guidance Needed for Any Future Conversions of Military Medical Positions to Civilian Positions*, Washington, D.C., GAO-08-370R, 2008.

———, *Human Capital: Further Actions Needed to Enhance DOD's Civilian Strategic Workforce Plan*, Washington, D.C., GAO-10-814R, 2010.

———, *DOD Civilian Personnel: Competency Gap Analyses and Other Actions Needed to Enhance DOD's Strategic Workforce Plans*, Washington, D.C., GAO-11-827T, 2011.

———, *DOD Needs Complete Assessments to Improve Future Civilian Strategic Workforce Plans*, Washington, D.C., GAO-12-1014, 2012.

———, *Additional Steps Needed to Help Determine the Right Size and Composition of DOD's Total Workforce*, Washington, D.C., GAO-13-470, 2013a.

———, *Critical Skills and Competency Assessments Should Help Guide DOD Civilian Workforce Decisions*, Washington, D.C., GAO-13-188, 2013b.

———, *Comprehensive and Updated Cost Savings Would Better Inform DOD Decision Makers If Future Civilian Furloughs Occur*, Washington, D.C., GAO-14-529, 2014a.

———, *DOD Should Fully Develop Its Civilian Strategic Workforce Plan to Aid Decision Makers*, Washington, D.C., GAO-14-565, 2014b.

U.S. Office of Personnel Management, *2013 Federal Employee Viewpoint Survey Results: Employees Influencing Change*, Department of Defense Agency Management Report, Washington, D.C., 2013.

———, *2015 Federal Employee Viewpoint Survey Results: Employees Influencing Change*, Department of Defense Agency Management Report, Washington, D.C., 2015.

Vernez, Georges, and H. G. Massey, *The Acquisition Cost-Estimating Workforce: Census and Characteristics*, Santa Monica, Calif.: RAND Corporation, TR-708-AF, 2009. As of May 1, 2016: http://www.rand.org/pubs/technical_reports/TR708.html

Werber, Laura, Lindsay Daugherty, Edward G. Keating, and Matthew Hoover, *An Assessment of the Civilian Acquisition Workforce Personnel Demonstration Project*, Santa Monica, Calif.: RAND Corporation, TR-1286-OSD, 2012. As of May 2, 2016: http://www.rand.org/pubs/technical_reports/TR1286.html

Whitley, John E., Brandon R. Gould, Nancy M. V. Huff, and Linda Wu, *Medical Total Force Management*, Alexandria, Va.: Institute for Defense Analyses, IDA Paper P-5047, 2014.

Wilson, Timothy, "Pentagon Should Cut Civilian, Not Military, Personnel," *The Hill*, April 3, 2014. As of August 10, 2015: http://thehill.com/blogs/congress-blog/homeland-security/202474-pentagon-should-cut-civilian-not-military-personnel

Other Laws, Regulations, Official Instructions, and Policy Guidance Relevant to Military-to-Civilian Conversions

Chairman of the Joint Chiefs of Staff, Joint Publication 4-10, *Operational Contract Support*, 2014.

Office of the Secretary of the Army, *Army Policy for Civilian Workforce Management and Service Contracts*, 2009.

United States Code, Title 10, Section 235, *Procurement of Contract Services: Specification of Amounts Requested in Budget*, January 3, 2012.

———, Title 10, Section 1597, *Civilian Positions: Guidelines for Reductions*, January 7, 2011.

———, Title 10, Section 2330, *Procurement of Contract Services: Management Structure*, January 3, 2012.

———, Title 10, Section 2383, *Contractor Performance of Acquisition Functions Closely Associated with Inherently Governmental Functions*, January 3, 2012.

———, Title 10, Section 2434, *Independent Cost Estimates: Operational Manpower Requirements*, January 7, 2011.

———, Title 10, Section 2462, *Reports on Public-Private Competition*, January 7, 2011.

———, Title 10, Section 2463, *Guidelines and Procedures for Use of Civilian Employees to Perform Department of Defense Functions*, January 3, 2012.

———, Title 10, Section 2465, *Prohibition on Contracts for Performance of Firefighting or Security-Guard Functions*, January 7, 2011.

Additional Reading on Military-to-Civilian Conversions and Related Issues

Asch, Beth J., *The Defense Civilian Workforce: Insights from Research*, testimony presented to the United States Senate Committee on Governmental Affairs, Subcommittee on Oversight of Government Management, Restructuring and the District of Columbia, Santa Monica, Calif.: RAND Corporation, CT-208, 2003. As of May 2, 2016: http://www.rand.org/pubs/testimonies/CT208.html

Barth, Thomas J., Stanley A. Horowitz, Mark F. Kaye, and Linda Wu, *Staffing Cyber Operations*, briefing to the Western Economics Association International, Alexandria, Va.: Institution for Defense Analysis, IDA Document D-5472, 2015.

Berman, Evan M., James S. Bowman, Jonathan P. West, and Montgomery R. Van Wart, *Human Resource Management in Public Service: Paradoxes, Processes, and Problems*, Los Angeles, Calif.: Sage Publications, 2012.

Bessler, Iric Brooke, *The Civilianization of Marine Corps Billets: A Methodology*, Monterey, Calif.: Naval Postgraduate School, thesis, 1989. As of August 4, 2015: http://www.dtic.mil/dtic/tr/fulltext/u2/a214736.pdf

Bigler, Julie K., *Sustaining the Future Civilian Workforce: DoD's Strategic Human Capital Management*, Washington, D.C.: Defense AT&L Special Edition, 2009.

Binkin, Martin, Herschel Kanter, and Rolf H. Clark, *Shaping the Defense Civilian Work Force: Economics, Politics, and National Security*, Washington, D.C.: Brookings Institution, 1978.

Bowman, Daniel R., *Civilianization Within the USAF Dental Corps—A Threat to Medical Readiness*, Maxwell Air Force Base, Al.: Air Command and Staff College, Air University, Student Paper Number 88-0340, 1988.

Calvert, Ken, "Secretary of Defense: 'We Can Reduce the Civilian Workforce,'" press release, Washington, D.C., March 4, 2015. As of April 16, 2015: http://calvert.house.gov/news/documentsingle.aspx?DocumentID=397423

Central All-Volunteer Force Task Force, *Civilian Substitution: A Report on Substitution of Civilians for Military Personnel in the Armed Forces*, Washington, D.C.: Office of the Assistant Secretary of Defense, Manpower and Reserve Affairs, 1972. As of August 4, 2015: http://www.dtic.mil/get-tr-doc/pdf?AD=AD0764523

Christensen, Eric W., Shayne Brannman, J. Sanders, Cori Rattelman, and Richard D. Miller, *Life-Cycle Costs of Selected Uniformed Health Professions*, Alexandria, Va: CNA, CRM D0006686.A3, April 2003.

Conaway, Donald G., Patricia B. Genung, and Joseph B. McMillan, *Military Leadership of Civilian Personnel: Achieving a Balance*, Cambridge, Mass.: Harvard University, Kennedy School of Government, research paper, 1996. As of August 4, 2015: http://www.dtic.mil/dtic/tr/fulltext/u2/a311162.pdf

Congressional Budget Office, *A Review of the Department of Defense's National Security Personnel System*, Washington, D.C.: Congressional Budget Office, Publication No. 3056, 2008.

Delaune, Elton J., and Roger R. Ramsey, *Civilian Substitution for Military Personnel: Concepts and Problems*, Carlisle Barracks, Pa.: U.S. Army War College, Research Paper, 1972.

Dunigan, Molly, Carrie M. Farmer, Rachel M. Burns, Alison Hawks, and Claude Messan Setodji, "Out of the Shadows: What We Know About the Well-Being and Experiences of Private Contractors Working in Conflict Environments," Santa Monica, Calif.: RAND Corporation, IG-111-RC, 2014. As of May 2, 2016:
http://www.rand.org/pubs/infographics/IG111.html

Eaglen, Mackenzie, "Cut the Pentagon's Civilian Workforce," *Breaking Defense*, April 30, 2014. As of April 6, 2015:
http://breakingdefense.com/2014/04/cut-the-pentagons-civilian-workforce/

Farrell, Brenda S., and John P. Hutton, "Competency Gap Analyses and Other Actions Needed to Enhance DOD's Strategic Workforce Plans," testimony before the Committee on Armed Services, House of Representatives, Washington, D.C.: U.S. Government Accountability Office, GAO-11-827T, 2011.

Fitzpatrick, Eric L., *A Study of the Feasibility and Benefits of Converting Certain Fleet Support Community Billets from Military to Civilian*, Monterey, Calif.: Naval Postgraduate School, thesis, 1998. As of August 4, 2015:
http://www.dtic.mil/get-tr-doc/pdf?AD=ADA346471

Garcia, Andrea, Hugo Keyner, Thomas J. Robillard, and Mary VanMullekom, "The Defense Acquisition Workforce Improvement Act: Five Years Later," *Acquisition Review Quarterly*, Summer 1997, pp. 295–314.

Gates, Susan M., Christine Eibner, and Edward G. Keating, "DoD Civilian Workforce Requirements," unpublished RAND Corporation research, 2004.

Gates, Susan M., Edward G. Keating, Adria Jewell, Lindsay Daugherty, Bryan Tysinger, and Ralph Masi, "The Department of the Navy's Civilian Acquisition Workforce," unpublished RAND Corporation research, 2008.

Gates, Susan M., and Christopher Paul, *Intern Programs as a Human Resources Management Tool for the Department of Defense*, Santa Monica, Calif.: RAND Corporation, MG-138-OSD, 2004. As of May 2, 2016:
http://www.rand.org/pubs/monographs/MG138.html

Gibbs, Michael, *Pay Competitiveness and Quality of Department Of Defense Scientists and Engineers*, Santa Monica, Calif.: RAND Corporation, MR-1312-OSD, 2001. As of May 2, 2016:
http://www.rand.org/pubs/monograph_reports/MR1312.html

Harlow, D. W., *Military to Civilian Conversion: Where Effectiveness Meets Efficiency*, Quantico, Va.: Command Staff College, Marine Corps University, EWS Contemporary Issue Paper, 2005. As of August 4, 2015:
http://www.dtic.mil/dtic/tr/fulltext/u2/a505641.pdf

Horowitz, Stanley A., Robert J. Atwell, and Shaun K. McGee, *Analyzing the Costs of Alternative Army Active/Reserve Force Mixes*, Alexandria, Va.: Institute for Defense Analyses, IDA Paper P-4884, 2012.

Kalleberg, Arne L., "Nonstandard Employment Relations: Part-Time, Temporary and Contract Work," *Annual Review of Sociology*, Vol. 26, 2000, pp. 341–365.

Keating, Edward G., *Cancellations and Delays in Completion of Department of Defense A-76 Cost Comparisons*, Santa Monica, Calif.: RAND Corporation, DB-191-OSD, 1997. As of May 2, 2016: http://www.rand.org/pubs/documented_briefings/DB191.html

Keating, Edward G., Frank Camm, and Christopher Hanks, *Sourcing Decisions for Air Force Support Services: Current and Historical Patterns*, Santa Monica, Calif.: RAND Corporation, DB-193-AF, 1997. As of May 2, 2016:
http://www.rand.org/pubs/documented_briefings/DB193.html

Kose, Bahadir S., *Civilian Substitution for Military Personnel: An Analysis of the Issues*, Monterey, Calif.: Naval Postgraduate School, thesis, 1990.

Levy, Robert A., Shing-Lai Cheng, and Patricia Netzer, *Attracting, Deploying, and Keeping Navy General Surgeons and Other Critical Wartime Specialists*, Alexandria, Va.: CNA, 2011.

Levy, Robert A., Eric W. Christensen, and Senanu Asamoah, *Raising the Bonus and the Prospects for DOD's Attracting Fully Trained Medical Personnel*, Alexandria, Va.: CNA, CRM D0013237.A2, February 2006.

Manuel, Kate M., and Jack Maskell, *Insourcing Functions Performed by Federal Contractors: Legal Issues*, Washington, D.C.: Congressional Research Service, R41810, 2013.

McGee, Shaun K., Lance M. Roark, Laila A. Wahedi, and Stanley A. Horowitz, *Active-Reserve Force Cost Model*, Alexandria, Va.: Institute for Defense Analyses, IDA Document D-5057, 2015.

Minnow, Martha, "Outsourcing Power: How Privatizing Military Efforts Challenges Accountability, Professionalism, and Democracy," *Boston College Law Review*, Vol. 46, No. 5, 2005, pp. 989–1026.

Morthole, Stuart E., *An Investigation of the Facets for Converting Military Authorizations for Maintenance Personnel to Civilian Positions*, Maxwell Air Force Base, Al.: Air Command and Staff College, Air University, Student Paper Number 84-1830, 1984.

Nataraj, Shanthi, Jessica M. Yeats, Frank A. Camm, and Lawrence M. Hanser, "The Future of the Army's Civilian Workforce: Comparing Projected Inventory with Anticipated Requirements and Estimating Cost Under Different Personnel Policies," unpublished RAND Corporation research, 2014.

Office of the Assistant Secretary of Defense (Manpower, Reserve Affairs and Logistics), *Civilian Substitution Potential*, Washington, D.C, May 3, 1977.

Office of Program Analysis and Evaluation, *The Economics of Sizing the Military Medical Establishment: Executive Report of the Comprehensive Study of the Military Medical Care System*, Washington, D.C.: Department of Defense, April 1994.

Office of the Secretary of Defense Cost Assessment and Program Evaluation, *Full Cost of Manpower Tool*. As of August 4, 2015:
https://fcom.cape.osd.mil/

Office of the Under Secretary of Defense, Personnel and Readiness, *Department of Defense Report on the Civilian and Military Mix in Support Occupations*, Report to the House Committee on National Security and Senate Committee on Armed Services, April 1995.

Rhode, Alfred S., Lewis Davis, and Richard E. Osseck, *Analysis of a Study Entitled 'Civilianization of Navy Fleet Support Ships*,' Arlington, Va.: Information Spectrum, Inc., ISI Report No. V-0514-02A, 1980.

Rhynedance, George H., *More Civilians on the West Point Faculty: Good for the Army, or Not?* Fort Leavenworth, Ks.: Army Command and General Staff College, thesis, 1993.

Schooner, Steven L., and Daniel S. Greenspahn, "Too Dependent on Contractors? Minimum Standards for Responsible Governance," *Journal of Contract Management*, 2008, pp. 9–25.

Schwartz, Moshe, and Jennifer Church, *Department of Defense's Use of Contractors to Support Military Operations: Background, Analysis, and Issues for Congress*, Washington, D.C.: Congressional Research Service, R43074, 2013.

Snyder, Don, Bernard Fox, Kristin F. Lynch, Raymond E. Conley, John A. Ausink, Laura Werber, William Shelton, Sarah A. Nowak, Michael R. Thirtle, and Albert A. Robbert, *Assessment of the Air Force Materiel Command Reorganization: Report for Congress*, Santa Monica, Calif.: RAND Corporation, RR-389-AF, 2013. As of May 2, 2016:
http://www.rand.org/pubs/research_reports/RR389.html

Stephenson-Tetu, Karen, *The Defense Civilian Workforce-Transformational Changes*, Carlisle Barracks, Pa.: United States Army War College, 2013.

U.S. Department of Defense Acquisition 2005 Task Force, *Shaping the Civilian Acquisition Workforce of the Future*, Washington, D.C.: Office of the Under Secretary of Defense, Technology, and Logistics, 2000.

U.S. Department of Defense, *Program Budget Decision 712*, December 24, 2003.

———, "Defense Budget Recommendation Statement," as prepared for delivery by Secretary of Defense Robert M. Gates, Arlington, Va., April 6, 2009.

———, *Quadrennial Defense Review Report*, February 2010.

———, *Strategic Management Plan: The Business of Defense FY2014–FY2015*, Washington, D.C., 2013. As of May 2, 2016:
http://dcmo.defense.gov/Portals/47/Documents/Publications/ASP/FY1415_SMP.pdf

U.S. Department of Homeland Security, *Balanced Workforce Strategy Guidance, Version 2.0*, Washington, D.C., 2011.

U.S. General Accounting Office, *DoD Force Mix Issues: Greater Reliance on Civilians in Support Roles Could Provide Significant Benefits*, Washington, D.C., NSIAD-95-5, 1994.

———, *A Self-Assessment Checklist for Agency Leaders*, Washington, D.C., OCG-00-14G, 2000.

———, *Acquisition Workforce: Department of Defense's Plans to Address Workforce Size and Structure Challenges*, Washington, D.C., GAO-02-630, 2002.

———, *DoD Personnel: DoD Actions Needed to Strengthen Civilian Human Capital Strategic Planning and Integration with Military Personnel and Sourcing Decisions*, Washington, D.C., GAO-03-475, 2003.

U.S. Government Accountability Office, *Defense Acquisitions: Continued Management Attention Needed to Enhance Use and Review of DOD's Inventory of Contracted Services*, Washington, D.C., GAO-13-491, 2013.

Wu, Linda, *Market Forces and Total Force Management: Military Medical Community*, Alexandria, Va.: Institute for Defense Analyses, IDA Document NS D-4918, 2013.

Zook, Aaron M., Jr., *Military Competency-Based Human Capital Management: A Step Toward the Future*, Carlisle Barracks, Pa.: United States Army War Project Strategy Research Project, 2006.